D0459956

LAS VEGAS
ENCOUNTER

SARA BENSON

Las Vegas Encounter
1st edition – May 2007

Published by Lonely Planet Publications Pty Ltd
ABN 36 005 607 983

Australia	Head Office, Locked Bag 1,
	Footscray, Vic 3011
	☎ 03 8379 8000 fax 03 8379 8111
	talk2us@lonelyplanet.com.au
USA	150 Linden St, Oakland, CA 94607
	☎ 510 893 8555 toll free 800 275 8555
	fax 510 893 8572
	info@lonelyplanet.com
UK	72–82 Rosebery Ave, Clerkenwell,
	London EC1R 4RW
	☎ 020 7841 9000 fax 020 7841 9001
	go@lonelyplanet.co.uk

This title was commissioned in Lonely Planet's Oakland office
and produced by: **Commissioning Editors** Suki Gear & Jennye
Garibaldi **Coordinating Editors** Kate James & Kyla Gillzan
Coordinating Cartographers Mandy Sierp & Anthony Phelan
Layout Designer Wibowo Rusli **Senior Editors** Helen Christinis
& Katie Lynch **Managing Cartographer** Alison Lyall **Cover
Designer** Jane Hart **Project Manager** Chris Love **Thanks to**
Nellie Bradley, Christi Braginton, David Burnett, Alyssa Bushey,
Amanda Canning, Laura Cleary, Sally Darmody, Jennifer Garrett,
Michelle Glynn, Michelle Mosbacher, Natalie Mounier, Wayne
Murphy, Sylke Neal-Finnegan, Adrianne Offermann, Stephanie
Pearson, Paul Piaia, Yvette Monet, Vivek Wagle, Celia Wood,
Wendy Wright

Photographs by Lonely Planet Images and Jerry Alexander
except for the following: p20 Holger Leue/Lonely Planet Images;
p39 Christina Lease/Lonely Planet Images; p41, p74, p116, p122
Sara Benson; p45 Charles Cook/Lonely Planet Images; p47 Curtis
Martin/Lonely Planet Images; p50, p66 Richard Cummins/Lonely
Planet Images; p51, p52, p138 Ray Laskowitz/Lonely Planet
Images; p143 Bill Bachmann/Lonely Planet Images; pp4–5,
p43 Las Vegas News Bureau/LVCVA; p49, p53 MGM Mirage.
Cover photograph Elvis impersonator, Las Vegas, Naki
Kouyioumtzis/Axiom.

All images are copyright of the photographers unless
otherwise indicated. Many of the images in this guide are
available for licensing from **Lonely Planet Images:** www
.lonelyplanetimages.com.

ISBN 978 1 74104 561 1

Printed through Colorcraft Ltd, Hong Kong.
Printed in China

HOW TO USE THIS BOOK

Color-Coding & Maps

Color-coding is used for symbols on maps and
in the text that they relate to (eg all eating
venues on the maps and in the text are given
a blue fork symbol).

Prices

Concession prices can include senior, student,
member or coupon discounts. Meal cost cat-
egories are listed on p91.

*Although the authors and Lonely Planet have taken
all reasonable care in preparing this book, we make
no warranty about the accuracy or completeness of
its content and, to the maximum extent permitted,
disclaim all liability arising from its use.*

SARA BENSON

First awestruck by the neon lights of the Strip during a cross-country trek from Chicago to California, Sara had a serendipitous one-night stand with Sin City that soon became a torrid love affair. Now she travels down to the Nevadan desert every chance she gets, and has racked up more time gambling, carousing and wandering around the Las Vegas Valley than she'll readily admit to her grandmother. She and her entourage have devoted many a lost weekend to indulging in hedonistic spas, nightclub hopping down the Strip and gambling until the bleary-eyed hours after  midnight in Glitter Gulch. She is an avid outdoor-sports enthusiast, too. Her writing has featured in magazines and newspapers across the USA, including the *Las Vegas Review-Journal*, *Los Angeles Times* and *National Geographic Adventure*. She is also the author of Lonely Planet's *Las Vegas* city guide.

SARA'S THANKS

Thanks to Andrew Dean Nystrom for his work on *Best of Las Vegas*.

THE PHOTOGRAPHER

Jerry Alexander enjoys most of his time in the Napa Valley, California. Once his vineyard is through the harvest he heads to his other home in Chiang Mai, Thailand. This is his sixth book for Lonely Planet.

Good images come from hard work and lots of help, and Thanaphon Yawirat supplied most of that help, always looking for that next image and not once losing her humor and positive outlook. It was much appreciated. Suki Gear in LP's Oakland office was there moving things forward every day we were in Las Vegas – thanks! Thanks also to the entire staff at MGM/Mirage public relations and the crew at Kirvin Doak.

Send us your Feedback | We love to hear from travelers – your comments keep us on our toes and help make our books better. Our well-traveled team reads every word on what you loved or loathed about this book. Although we cannot reply individually to postal submissions, we always guarantee that your feedback goes straight to the appropriate authors, in time for the next edition – and the most useful submissions are rewarded with a free book. To send us your updates – and find out about Lonely Planet events, newsletters and travel news – visit our award-winning website: *lonelyplanet.com/feedback*.

Note: We may edit, reproduce and incorporate your comments in Lonely Planet products such as guidebooks, websites and digital products, so let us know if you don't want your comments reproduced or your name acknowledged. For a copy of our privacy policy visit *lonelyplanet.com/privacy*.

CONTENTS

THE AUTHOR	03
THIS IS LAS VEGAS	07
LAS VEGAS LAYOUT	09
HIGHLIGHTS	10
ITINERARIES	27
GAMBLING & CASINOS	32
SEE | SHOP | EAT | PLAY	62
>SEE	65
>SHOP	79
>EAT	91
>PLAY	119
OUT OF TOWN	143
BACKGROUND	149
DIRECTORY	160
INDEX	171
MAPS	177

JIMMY CHOO

Other clubs only give you half the view.
TOTALLY NUDE REVUE
Open 24 Hours • 2580 S. Highland
SHERI'S CABARET

THIS IS LAS VEGAS

Vegas is the ultimate escape. As ambitious as a starlet vying for your affections, the USA's fastest-growing metropolis and its glamorous megaresorts stand ready to cater to your every whim 24/7. A few frenzied sleepless nights here are more intoxicating than a week-long bender anywhere else.

Be as naughty as you want, pretend to be someone else entirely and watch your most devilish fantasies become real. Let the everyday rules of behavior slide a little, like a burlesque dancer's feather boa. Chill. Sin City stands ready to give you an alibi: what happens in Vegas, stays in Vegas. Who can resist such outrageous temptation? Not you, not me.

This city demands a suspension of disbelief; so don't take it too seriously. A Bible-toting Elvis kisses a giddy couple that just pledged eternity in the Chapel ovf Love. A blue-haired grandma feeds nickels into a slot machine while chain smoking and slugging gin-and-tonics. A porn star saunters by a nightclub's velvet rope. Blink, and you'll miss it. Sleep? Fuhgeddaboudit.

In Sin City, fate is decided by the spin of a roulette wheel. It's a place where lucky schmucks are treated like royalty and the rich lose thousands in an instant. It doesn't matter if you play the penny slots or drop a bankroll at the poker tables – it's no gamble that you'll have the time of your life here.

Vegas wasn't built to last, but ironically it does. This high-octane desert capital has survived the mischief and mayhem of mobsters like Bugsy Siegel, mushroom clouds from atomic bomb blasts, rock 'n' roll mania for Elvis, the eccentricities of billionaire Howard Hughes and, most recently, the implosion of landmark Rat Pack casino hotels. Perhaps Rome's not the Eternal City – Vegas is.

What matters is that, like an oasis mirage in a parched desert, Las Vegas is whatever you desire most, if only for a day, a night or a dirty weekend. Here, everyone lives like the King.

Top left Forum Shops (p80), Caesars Palace **Top right** 'Motown' Vegas-style **Bottom** On the streets of Las Vegas

LAS VEGAS LAYOUT

Sprawled immodestly along Las Vegas Blvd, the **Strip** is constantly rein-
venting itself, becoming ever more spectacular (and more of a spectacle). Every monolithic megaresort is an attraction, with plenty of action
besides gambling. It runs south past Mandalay Bay toward the airport
and north all the way to the Stratosphere. Its G-spot is the intersection
with Flamingo Blvd.

Downtown presides over the distant north end of the tourist corridor,
with **Glitter Gulch** (and the canopied Fremont Street Experience) streaking
down its middle. The city's historic quarter is preferred by serious gamblers, who find faux volcanoes beneath them; the smoky, low-ceilinged
casinos have changed little over the years. Recently, however, the area
has been undergoing a renaissance of cool – stay tuned.

The desolate stretch of Las Vegas Blvd between downtown and the
Strip is nicknamed the **Naked City**. These downtrodden streets are stuffed
with tattered cheap motels, strip clubs, tattoo parlors and drive-thru
wedding chapels. The **Gateway Arts District**, blossoming around the intersection with Charleston Blvd, is for hipsters, artists and alt-cultural types.

The strip malls of the **Eastside** and **Westside** are the domains of locals,
while the area around the **University of Nevada** (UNLV) campus attracts
youthful carpetbaggers. Anchored by the Las Vegas Convention Center,
Paradise Rd streams south into the flamboyant **Fruit Loop** area, the epi-
center of the lesbigay community.

Disorientation is a constant risk, whether you're searching for your
hotel room, stumbling drunkenly through a casino or desperately trying
to remember where you parked the damn car.

Navigating Vegas

	South Strip	Center Strip	North Strip	Downtown
South Strip	n/a	monorail 5min	monorail 15min	taxi 25min
Center Strip	monorail 5min	n/a	monorail 10min	taxi 20min
North Strip	monorail 15min	monorail 10min	n/a	taxi 15min
Downtown	taxi 25min	taxi 20min	taxi 15min	n/a

Left All dressed up, on the streets of Vegas

>HIGHLIGHTS

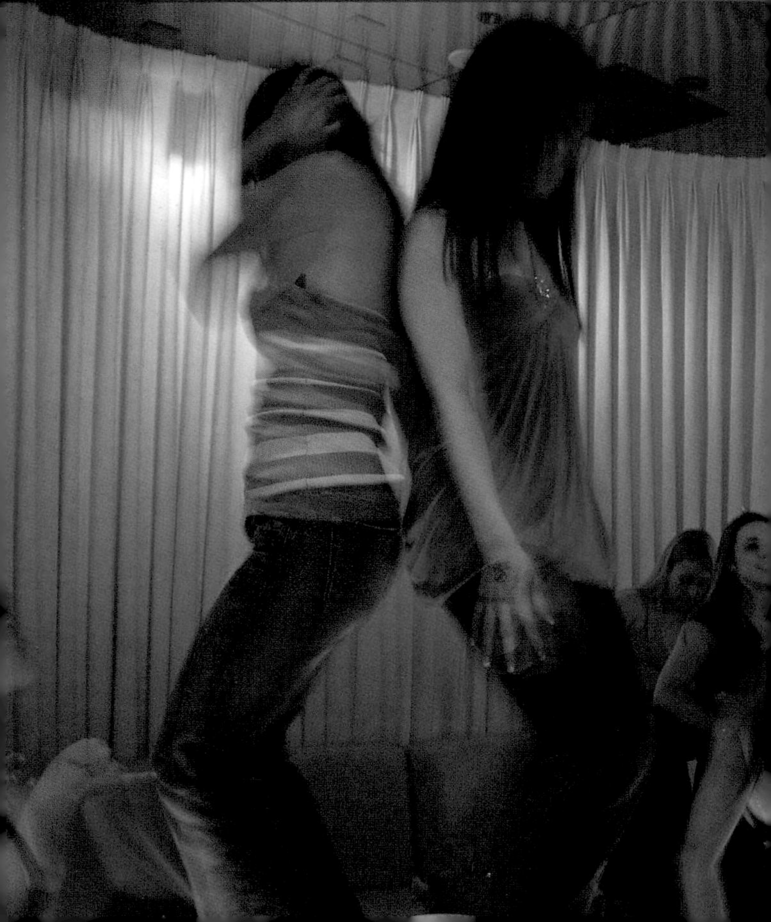

>1 Cruising the Strip — 12
>2 Gorging at a buffet — 13
>3 Betting the farm — 14
>4 Lazing by the pool — 15
>5 Finding vintage Vegas — 16
>6 Cheesy, cheapo Las Vegas — 18
>7 Splashing out at a spa — 20
>8 Partying hard — 21
>9 Getting high — 22
>10 Tying the knot — 24
>11 Hiding out in your hotel — 26

Tangerine (p130), TI (Treasure Island)

>1 CRUISING THE STRIP

GETTING A SENSORY OVERLOAD ON THE WORLD'S FLASHIEST BOULEVARD

If it's your first time visiting Vegas and you're driving, make sure you do a few things. First, arrive after dark. Next, pull over and admire everything from afar before you hit the high-speed city limits. Finally, exit off the interstate and cruise the length of Las Vegas Blvd (aka the Strip). Your eyes will pop out of your head, guaranteed.

Flashing neon welcomes those weary from their interminably long trip across the desert (or equally taxing flight across the continent or an ocean) and gives 'em glorious sensory overload. From the beacon shooting toward the stars out of the Darth-Vader dark pyramid of the Luxor (p47) to the Big Apple cityscape of New York-New York (p49), the thousands of feather-like pink bulbs adorning the venerable Flamingo (p46), the spritzing musical fountains of Bellagio (p71), the Mirage's exploding volcano (p71) and the gigantic Stratosphere Tower (p70), all of the Strip is a spectacle.

Not that you have to drive it, of course. You can hoof it, though it'll mightily tire out your tootsies. Or cycle it, skateboard it, bodysurf it, roar down it on a Harley hog or even (as we saw one funny stuntman doing) rise above it all on a pair of rickety stilts. Watching – or joining the ranks of – the crazy folks is all part of the fun right here on the infamous Las Vegas Strip.

>2 GORGING AT A BUFFET
EATING YOUR FILL (OR MORE) AT A CASINO HOTEL

If things haven't gone your way in the poker room, or when you've thrown the dice the wrong way at the craps table, or after every pull of the slot-machine lever comes up short, you can still feel like you're winning the jackpot simply by feasting at one of Vegas' dozens of buffets (see the boxed text, p93).

Veterans of 'groaning boards' proffer some sage words of advice. First, starve yourself for as long as possible before saddling up at a buffet, and don't count on eating any meals afterward. Breakfast or lunch – or better yet weekend bunch – is better value than dinner, unless special entrées such as steak or seafood are added. And the predictable principle usually applies: the more expensive the casino hotel, the better the fare. Think Wynn, Bellagio etc.

Once you wait out the queue, the time-tested strategy is to steal teensy servings of absolutely everything before deciding what you really want to eat. Why get stuck with soggy sushi when a smiling chef is making fresh omelettes and crepes just a few food stations over? And always save room for multiple mini desserts, from floating islands of caramel meringue to house-made gelato.

Oh, and leave behind a tip (p169) for the servers who bussed all those gluttonous piles of scrap-ridden plates off your table. Without them, you'd have drowned in those foodstuffs.

>3 BETTING THE FARM
PUTTING YOUR FORTUNE IN THE HANDS OF FATE

Las Vegas wouldn't exist if people didn't come seeking their fortunes in the green felt jungle. From 19th-century silver miners and bordello prostitutes, to the New York mafia and billionaire Howard Hughes, to online gambling geeks who hang in until the final table at the World Series of Poker, a lucky few have made a mint here.

Advertising billboards around town are plastered with the smiling faces of Marge and David 'who just won $25,000 on our hot, hot slots!', which may seduce you into trying your hand at gaming. Maybe someone hands you the dice at the craps table, and you can't resist giving 'em a to-die-for roll. Or you plug a quarter into the video poker machine and you're dealt a royal flush. Once you've caught the fever after a gigantic pay-off, there may be almost no going back.

Statistically speaking, however, the casino (aka 'the house') pretty much always has an edge over the gambler. Not even blackjack is really a 'beatable' game. So before you bet your precious nest egg on the random turn of Fate's roulette wheel, do your homework. Turn to p32 for the lowdown on casinos and the most popular games.

BEST HIGH-LIMIT CASINOS

> Wynn (p44)
> Mirage (p42)
> Bellagio (p38)
> Venetian (p43)
> Mansion at MGM Grand (p40)

>4 LAZING BY THE POOL
LOSING YOURSELF IN FANTASTIC WATER WORLDS

Las Vegas thrives on its pop culture of excess. Ever since casino impresario Steve Wynn launched the fabulous Polynesian-themed casino hotel the Mirage at the end of the no-limits 1980s, every megaresort has aimed to be the biggest and best.

And that rule applies to swimming pools, too. Nothing has proved too difficult to dream or achieve. Mandalay Bay imported thousands of pounds of Southern California sand to build its artificial beach, where board-riders surf on manufactured waves. The MGM Grand designed a 1000ft (300m) lazy river ride, where guests float along by barely moving a muscle. At Caesars Palace's Garden of the Gods Oasis, goddesses proffer frozen grapes, and topless sunbathing (ooh, la la!) is allowed at the Venus pool.

It all started with the Flamingo, of course, the Strip's first movie star–worthy casino hotel. Out back you can still glimpse its 1940s-era waterfalls, lagoons and grottoes where pink flamingos strike a pose. Nowadays, though, the bad boys and girls hang out at the Hard Rock, reclining inside grass-shack cabañas with personal misting systems and playing swim-up blackjack at the exotic Palapa pavilion. Other sexy scenes are found at the Palms, where the pool has a pink-tinted floor, and in the 50-person party hot tub at TI (Treasure Island).

For a rundown of Vegas' coolest swimming pools, see p123.

>5 FINDING VINTAGE VEGAS
SEARCHING OUT SOME RETRO VEGAS COOL

If you've already been dazzled by the Strip and gotten down-and-dirty in ol' downtown, it's time to go straight to the source of those Rat Pack–era vibes. Though in a town that moves as fast as this one, priceless pieces of history get lost, bulldozed, imploded and discarded every day. So devote a little time to unraveling the past in the present.

You just have to know where to look. Start by driving by that famous 'Welcome to Fabulous Las Vegas' sign (see the boxed text, p65) south of the Strip. Snap a souvenir photo of yourself standing in the median strip, and zoom back up Las Vegas Blvd.

Then saunter into the Strip's original glam casino hotel, the Flamingo (p46), the folly that Bugsy built. Check out the yesteryear photos of movie stars and mobsters by the valet parking stand. Nearby at Bally's, catch a cheesy *Jubilee!* topless show (p137) after taking a behind-the-scenes tour led by a real showgirl or chorus boy (p168). Find out: how *do* they manage to keep all those rhinestones so strategically placed?

Detour east of the Strip to the Liberace Museum (p75; pictured right) to gawk at the outlandish costumes once worn by this legendary Vegas entertainer. As you keep gallivanting around town, look out for Elvis impersonators or play blackjack with a 'dealertainer' dressed like the King at the Imperial Palace (p75).

With the perpetual demolition and construction along the Strip, not much more of old Vegas remains. But the closer you get to downtown, the more relics you'll see. Take Las Vegas Blvd, which beelines past old-fashioned strip clubs (p134) and wedding chapels (p76) galore. Or follow Main St past Rainbow Feather Co (p88), where showgirls' boas are made of exotic feathers and dyed by hand, and

THE FIRST CARPET JOINT
The legendary Fremont has been packing 'em in since 1956, when it opened as downtown's first high-rise. Separating it from the pack was its wall-to-wall carpeting – all the nearby casinos had sawdust-covered floors. It was here, too, that lounge singer Wayne Newton launched his long-standing career.

the Gamblers General Store (p82), which stocks decks of playing cards retired from famous-name casinos.

Downtown's Fremont St is the heart of yesteryear's Glitter Gulch. Look up for the classic neon signs, Vegas Vic and Vegas Vicky, still standing tall. The Golden Gate casino hotel (p55) has been encouraging vice here since 1900. Down side alleys off Fremont St, take a sneak peek at other vintage neon signs, all courtesy of the Neon Museum (p76), based inside the Neonopolis.

Bravely finish off your tour of old-school Vegas at the El Cortez casino hotel (p54), which has barely changed a lick since the 1940s. Or get romantic back on the Strip at the Peppermill casino's flickering Fireside Lounge (p120), which has been inspiring couples to make whoopee for decades.

>6 CHEESY, CHEAPO LAS VEGAS

JOINING THE LOW ROLLERS IN THE LAND THAT TASTE FORGOT

Some critics lament that everything in Las Vegas is in outrageously bad taste, and, of course, that's almost 100% true. But that's actually something to celebrate. It's as much fun to dive into the city's unbelievably campy depths as it is to aim for its snobbish heights of luxury.

You could spend all day watching the gob-stopping free casino spectaculars (p70) and inhaling the (almost free) food and drinks. Did you know they'll serve you free booze even if you're just playing the 'Penny Alley' slot machines? It's true.

If you're rarin' to go for a low-roller's ride through Las Vegas, there's no better place to start than downtown's Fremont St. Grab a 99¢ electric-blue-colored margarita in a souvenir 3ft-high plastic glass, buy a tacky T-shirt from a 'Sin City' souvenir shop and stagger around dive casinos while the Fremont Street Experience's cheesy laser-light show (p71) flashes overhead. Fight for a seat next to the blue-haired grannies inside the Plaza (p58) bingo room or quaff cocktails inside the casino's glass-domed Center Stage bar, where you can pretend to rise above the hoi polloi.

On the North Strip, a few kitschy casino hotel hold-outs from the 1950s and '60s still survive. Circus Circus (p54), which Hunter S Thompson thought was best experienced while high out of one's mind, wins the prize for the cheesiest casino theme. Pick up a 'fun book' full of discount coupons to redeem at laughably bad Slots-A-Fun (p76) next door. Across the street, grab a tiki drink at the neon-lit

VEGAS' MOST KITSCHY SOUVENIRS

> Casino-themed cocktail glass (eg plastic Eiffel Tower from Paris-Las Vegas, colorful ceramic showgirl from Bally's)
> Skimpy G-string, platform go-go boots or an erotic toy from a naughty novelty shop (p87)
> Showgirls' feather boa from Rainbow Feather Co (p88)
> Casino paraphernalia from the Gamblers General Store (p88)
> Anything that costs a buck or less from Bonanza Gifts (p88)

Fireside Lounge (p120) inside the Peppermill casino. Are you boozed enough yet to keep enjoying this?

Moving down the Strip, nothing could be tackier than the new Sirens of TI show (p72), where curvaceous pirates are outfitted in Victoria's Secret-esque lingerie. Keep the fantasy mind/jet going inside the live-action Madame Tussauds Las Vegas (p75), where you can pretend to marry movie stars or match skills with a sports legend. Or you can snap a photo of yourself with a celebrity impersonator at the Imperial Palace (p75), then sweet talk a toga-clad cocktail waitress at Caesars Palace (p39) or a showgirl at Bally's (p54) into posing for one, too. Ladies, your knight in shining armor awaits at Excalibur, surely one of the Strip's most ridiculous casino hotels.

Last but not least, don't forget to pay your respects to the maestro of flamboyant kitsch, Liberace, at the off-Strip museum (p75) where fanatical 'Red Hats' keep the candles of his outrageous shrine burning bright.

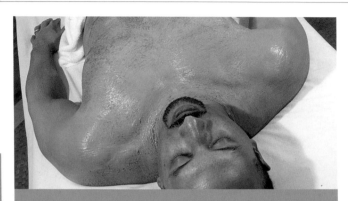

>7 SPLASHING OUT AT A SPA
TAKING A BREAK AT A DESERT OASIS

Now more than ever, visiting Las Vegas is about much more than mere gambling. A stopover these days is about the headlong, hedonistic pursuit of pleasure in all of its myriad varieties, so it was inevitable that fantastic spas would blossom here.

Las Vegas (Spanish for 'the meadows') has been an oasis in the Mojave Desert for millennia. Although its springs don't directly feed any of the city's 21st-century spas, that hardly matters. You can still find rejuvenation in just about any casino-hotel spa. Competition among the megaresorts is fierce, with indulgence ante happily being upped by every new spa on the block …er, the Strip.

Seeking Hawaiian hot stone, Indian ayurvedic or Thai massage? Classes in rock climbing, kickboxing and sunrise yoga? Cocktail-flavored body scrubs and floral facials? Or 'aromapothecary' showers, blissful hydrotherapy circuits and co-ed tropical waterfall hot tubs? Nothing is too exotic. If it can be imagined, it can be experienced here. Some spas are even open 24 hours. Others specialize in tempting 'detox' treatments for the morning after that midnight madness.

So what are you waiting for? Treat yourself. You just might feel reborn.

For highly recommended spas, see p123.

>8 PARTYING HARD

HITTING THE NIGHTCLUBS AND DANCING TIL YOU DROP

Booze, bodacious bodies and booty are what many come to Vegas for, since a drunken crawl along the Strip is just what the witch doctor ordered. The beautiful thing about Sin City is that you don't have to wait until a civilized cocktail hour to start carousing. Champagne brunches can start the morning off with a bang, some bars stay open 24/7, nightclubs rev up even on weekdays, and after-hours parties keep going strong until oh, about noon.

The launching pad of choice for a wild Vegas night is a svelte 'ultra lounge' (p128) on the Strip, where cocktails are mixed tableside by models, eye-popping burlesque dancers shimmy or sky-high views are the specialty of the house.

But these are mere stepping stones to Vegas' premier nightclubs (p130), pure fantasyland environments where sin is hawk in style. DJs as gorgeous as deep house mixes, go-go girls covered by little more than flower petals, and plush VIP bottle-service booths are all indulgently over-the-top. Or catch a famous rock star's show at The Joint or House of Blues (p125).

There's no sleep for the wicked, of course, not even after 4am. Some choose to escape into the arms of G-string babes at off-Strip strip clubs (p134), while others head for hipster watering holes at the edges of downtown (p120). Wherever you wind up, feasting on a steak before dawn is a late-night Vegas must (see the boxed text, p110).

>9 GETTING HIGH
LOOKING OUT PAST THE GLITTERING CITY FROM THE STRATOSPHERE TOWER

After a sweaty day traipsing up and down the Strip, especially when the dog days of summer hit, there's no better heat relief than to whoosh up the Stratosphere Tower courtesy of the USA's fastest elevators. There, almost 1150ft (350m) above the ground, strong breezes make the air cooler, not to mention clearer. On a good day, it's a cinch to see for many miles across the entire valley encircled by peaked mountains.

The eagle's-eye city skyline view can make anyone feel as rich as a casino mogul, especially while knocking back stiff martinis at the Romance at Top of the World lounge (p129). But that's not the only way to get high atop the Stratosphere Tower. The pointed pinnacle of the city's tallest building is designed with thrill rides (p70), including the

aptly named Insanity (pictured above), which swings riders out 60ft (18m) away from the edge of the tower into thin air, then spins its huge claw arms that elevate to a 70° angle. Or try the Big Shot, which really gets blood rushing by rocketing riders in outward-facing seats up and down a steel spire.

Whether you show up for sunset or star gazing, nothing tops this vista.

TOP FIVE VIEWS OF VEGAS
> Stratosphere Tower (p70)
> Mix ultra lounge (p129)
> Eiffel Tower (p68)
> ghostbar (p128)
> McCarran International Airport (p160) – in the Terminal 1 short-term parking garage, take the elevator to level 6. Bring quarters to feed the parking meters!

>10 TYING THE KNOT
GETTING HITCHED IN SIN CITY

Heaven might not be your place, but 'Marriages Made in *Las Vegas*' definitely doesn't have the same ring to it. But there must be something magical about it; on average one couple ties the knot every five minutes in Sin City. Wedding services range from a 10-minute drive-thru at a downtown chapel to a big, all-out 'do' at a glam casino megaresort.

The wild, wacky reasons people cite for getting hitched here are countless, but low licensing fees and the absence of waiting-period and blood-test requirements are the most often mentioned. Also, the 50-50 odds of a marriage surviving 'till death do us part' start to look pretty damn good in comparison to the chances of hitting a royal flush at the poker table. By the way, you don't have to be sober to get married here either. That helps some folks a lot.

Choices for the perfect spot to say 'I do' are endless. Weddings are performed in gondolas at the Venetian (p43), inside the Stratosphere's Chapel in the Clouds (p52), or atop the Eiffel Tower (p68) at Paris-Las Vegas. You can hire an Elvis impersonator to serenade you with 'Blue Hawaii,' or dress up like Marilyn Monroe. Sci-fi geeks proclaim their undying love to the galaxy at Star Trek: The Experience (p76). You can even get married on the floor of the Grand Canyon – or completely nekkid.

Of course, to be truthful, the more Vegas wedding chapels you see, the less you may be inclined to entrust them with the happiest day of your lives. Many are pretty tacky, full of plastic flowers, fake stained-glass windows and doll's-house pews. You may feel rushed,

MADE IN HEAVEN...OR NOT?
Among the scores of celebrity couples who have exchanged vows in Las Vegas are Elvis Presley and Priscilla Beaulieu, Cindy Crawford and Richard Gere, Bruce Willis and Demi Moore, and Angelina Jolie and Billy Bob Thornton. Only half of all marriages made in Las Vegas last, of course. Notoriously short-lived promises made by the likes of Britney Spears (a 55-hour marriage) have spurred Clark County to send follow-up letters to newlyweds later in the mail, asking if they *really* meant to get married or not.

too, as these places crank out dozens of weddings every day. Expect to pay upwards of $200 for a basic service, including a chintzy limo ride to the chapel if you're lucky.

Be advised that New Year's Eve and Valentine's Day are crush times for Vegas wedding chapels, so plan ahead if you want to say your vows on either of these days. You can apply for the required marriage license online up to a year in advance. For details on licensing and popular wedding chapels, see p76. Even if you're not contemplating tying the knot yourself, it's still worth a peek inside a wedding chapel to see if anyone else is crazy enough to do it. Wish 'em luck!

>11 HIDING OUT IN YOUR HOTEL
ROOM SERVICE IS ONLY THE BEGINNING

It's true that Vegas is a city that's rushing with adrenaline 24/7. But sometimes the best thing to do is nothing at all – in the luxury surrounds of your own hotel room.

Sleeping in late is required for party animals who were out gambling, club hopping and making merry mayhem till dawn. You'll find Vegas hotel rooms have the most creative, collectible versions of 'Do Not Disturb' signs; the one in the MGM Grand's West Wing simply states 'Recharging.'

There's very little that's not available in a minibar or on a room-service menu somewhere in this city. At the Hard Rock, you can order Love Jones lingerie and erotic play boxes (whoa, handcuffs!) delivered straight to your room. Champagne on ice is available at even low-rollers' hotels, but how many will also deliver a gourmet hot-fudge sundae at 3am like the Luxor?

The plushest casino hotels in Vegas (think: Wynn, Venetian, Caesars Palace, Bellagio) have exclusive all-suites towers with VIP concierges and every imaginable amenity, making sure no one would ever want to leave. For a hipper hotel getaway, the mod high-tech suites at THEhotel at Mandalay Bay have plasma TVs and deep soaking tubs – in the same room! Elsewhere, naughty bachelors/bachelorettes and their entourages won't be able to resist the Palms' playpen suites.

For more advice on where to stay, see p163.

ITINERARIES

ONE DAY

Speed from the airport to the Strip in a stretch limo. Check in at your hotel, or just drop off your bags, then head for the poker tables. Gawk at the Strip's fabulous free attractions (p30) and shopping arcades as you stroll through its opulent megaresorts (p32), such as the Bellagio, Caesars Palace, Venetian and MGM Grand. Use double-decker Deuce buses (p161) or the monorail (p162) to bounce along Las Vegas Blvd. Dine at a top chef's table (p91), then party at Sin City's hottest nightclubs (p130) until the sun comes up. After a quick cat nap, hit a big breakfast buffet before catching your flight out.

ONE WEEKEND

Fly into Vegas on Friday. Follow the one-day itinerary above, but without rushing. Fire up your first night at one of the Strip's ultra lounges and wind it down before dawn at an after-hours DJ club (p128).

Sleep late the next morning. Laze by the pool (p15), take a gambling lesson or indulge at a primo spa (p123). Drive to Red Rock Canyon (p146) for sunset, then detour downtown to neon-lit Glitter Gulch. As midnight rolls around, boomerang back to the Strip for more insane nightlife (p119).

Wake up to an indulgent Sunday brunch (see the boxed text, p93), then gamble like crazy until the last minute (even the airport has slot machines!).

THREE DAYS

Cover everything described in the one-day and one-weekend itineraries above. But also make time for a trip out of town, either to the awesome Grand Canyon (p145) or nearby Hoover Dam (p144), followed by a scenic drive around Lake Mead into the Valley of Fire. On your first or last day, queue up before noon at a half-price ticket booth (see the boxed text, p119) for tickets to a comedy, music or dance show or, if you're lucky, a sold-out production show (p136). That same afternoon, detour off the beaten tourist path to the Atomic Testing Museum (p66) or to browse a few quirky only-in-Vegas boutique shops (p88).

Left Fremont Street Experience (p71) **Previous** Rio casino hotel (p60)

ITINERARIES

HIGH ROLLIN' HEDONISM

Cruise the Strip (p12) in a cherry-red convertible and hit the high-stakes tables for a taste of the casino action. After sunset, dine with a star chef (p91), then mingle with Hollywood celebrities at an ultra lounge (p128) and party till dawn in a red-hot nightclub's VIP room. Wake up around noon. Start off with a champagne buffet (see the boxed text, p93). Soak up the desert sun by a sexy pool scene (p15) or luxuriate at a primo spa (p20). Take an Italian sports car for a test drive after bagging the latest fashions from Milan, Paris and Tokyo at the Strip's megaresorts (p80). Peep at a burlesque show after dark (p128).

VINTAGE VEGAS

Pay your respects to 1940s mobsters by rolling the dice at the Flamingo casino hotel (p46), then detour downtown to Glitter Gulch to see where it all began. Stroll down Fremont St, peering at its open-air museum of vintage neon signs. Sidle up to a low-limit table at a classy carpet joint like the glittering Golden Nugget (p56). Play some poker in the back room at Binion's (p45), the first casino to offer no-limit Texas Hold'em. Stop by the courthouse before getting hitched at a kitschy wedding chapel (p24), Vegas-style! Celebrate your newfound bliss with a retro cocktail at the Peppermill's Fireside Lounge (p120).

FORWARD PLANNING

Three weeks before you go Start surfing some key Las Vegas websites (see p166) and dabbling in the local media (p167); score tickets for any major concerts, production shows or sporting events that catch your eye (p119); book a table at a superstar chef's restaurant (p91).

One week before you go Call your hotel (p163) to check if room prices have dropped, and if they have, request that your reservation rate be lowered, too – you can save hundreds of dollars that way; make an appointment at one of the Strip's unisex spas (p123) or for an out-of-town adventure tour (p148).

The day before you go Reconfirm your flight and print out your hotel and car-rental reservations; check online to find out about the hottest nightclubs and live entertainment; then get loads of extra sleep – after you arrive in Sin City, you'll desperately need it!

FOR FREE

When you're down to the felt (ie your last dime), don't despair. Some of Vegas' most amusing diversions don't cost a thing. Popular low-roller attractions include the Bellagio's dancing fountains (p38), the Mirage's exploding volcano (p42), the Sirens of TI pirate battle at Treasure Island (p53), the MGM Grand's lion habitat (p72), the wildlife gardens at the Flamingo (p46), high-wire circus acts inside Circus Circus (p54) and celebrity impersonators at the Imperial Palace (p57). Detour to the Hard Rock casino (p56), where priceless rock 'n' roll memorabilia adorns the casino walls. Downtown boasts the tacky Fremont Street Experience (p71).

> Bellagio   38
> Caesars Palace   39
> MGM Grand   40
> Mirage   42
> Venetian   43
> Wynn   44
> Binion's   45
> Flamingo   46
> Luxor   47
> Mandalay Bay   48
> New York-New York   49
> Paris-Las Vegas   50
> Sahara   51
> Stratosphere   52
> TI (Treasure Island)   53
> Other Casinos   54

Rio casino hotel (p60)

GAMBLING & CASINOS

Gambling can be an exhilarating experience – every lucky roll of the dice gives an electrifying rush – but when it comes to Vegas casinos, it's important to remember one thing: the house advantage. In every game except poker, the house has a statistical winning edge (the 'percentage') over the gambler, and for nearly every payout in nearly every game, the house 'holds' a small portion of the winnings.

Amounts vary with the game and with individual bets, but over the long haul, you're guaranteed to lose everything that you gamble. Think of gambling only as entertainment for which you pay a fee. Understand the games you're playing, don't bet more than you're prepared to lose and learn to leave when you're 'up' (ahead).

Traditional casino games include poker, blackjack, baccarat, craps, roulette and slot machines. You must be at least 21 years old to play. Every game has its own customs, traditions and strategies. Almost all casinos can give you guides that show how to play the game and may offer free gaming lessons. It's OK to ask your dealer for help and advice. For instance, the dealer can tell you what the strategy is for the blackjack hand you've just been dealt. It's polite to 'toke,' or tip, the dealer if you are winning. Either place a chip on the layout (the area where you place your bet) for the dealer to take, or place a side bet for the dealer to collect.

Poker has become the hottest game in town. Fueled by seemingly endless TV coverage and the explosion of online play, would-be legends are flocking to the tables, ready to test their cunning and grit against other hometown heroes and touring pros. Most card rooms take only a small percentage of each pot, leaving the vast majority of the money to be won and lost by the players themselves. Poker betting comes in three basic

Left Hooters casino hotel (p57)

TOP FIVE POKER ROOMS

> Wynn (p44) – Vegas' poshest poker room
> Bellagio (p38) – where the World Poker Tour finals happen
> Mirage (p42) – the Strip's ground-breaking poker room 'remixed'
> Binion's (p45) – the ex-Horseshoe pushed the limits of Texas Hold'em
> Rio (p60) – home of the World Series of Poker

flavors: limit, no-limit, and pot limit. While it's not the only game in town, Texas Hold'em is far and away the most common.

While poker may be grabbing the headlines, **blackjack** (aka '21') remains far and away the most popular table game Vegas has to offer. Players love blackjack for all kinds of reasons. It's relatively simple to master its basic strategies. There's easy camaraderie with sociable dealers. Casinos offer comps – freebies like meals, shows, even luxury suites – to those willing to gamble a substantial amount of money. Almost every player has had the experience of making an absolute killing at the table, leading them to feel blackjack is a 'beatable' game. But not all blackjack games are created equal, and every casino lays down its own set of rules.

Nothing conjures the image of high stakes, black tuxedoes and James Bond like **baccarat**, and yet, of the card games, it possesses the least strategy – none, in fact. The rules are fixed, and there are no decisions for the player except for how to bet. High minimum bets ensure that only those with large bankrolls sit down to play.

A lively, fast-paced **craps** table has players shouting, crowds gathering and everyone hoping for that lucky 'hot' streak of the dice. Even though the odds are exactly the same on every roll, that doesn't stop people from betting their 'hunches' and believing that certain numbers are 'due.' Because the betting possibilities are complicated, and shift as play continues, it's important to spend some time studying a betting guide and begin playing with the simplest wager, on the pass/don't pass line, which also happens to be one of the better bets in a Vegas casino.

The ancient game of **roulette** is easy to understand and hypnotic to play. Roulette provides the most clear demonstration of the house edge. The roulette wheel has 38 numbers – from 1 to 36, plus 0 and 00 (European roulette wheels typically do not have '00,' which makes the American version much harder). The layout is marked with the numbers and various betting combinations. Most bets pay off at even money, but the chances of a win are less than 50%, because the 0 and 00 don't count as odd or even, red or black, high or low. These aren't the best odds in the casino, but they're far from the worst.

Simplest of all are **slot machines** – you put in money and pull the handle (or push a button) – and they're wildly popular. A player can have no effect on the outcome. The probabilities are programmed into the machine, and the chances of winning are the same on every pull. If you hit the jackpot, wait by the machine until an attendant arrives.

Popular with locals, **video poker** games are often built into a bar. By employing correct strategy and finding machines with the best payout schedules, it's possible to improve your chances of winning. Look for machines that reward a pair of jacks or better, and have a one-coin payout of nine coins for a full house and six coins for a flush.

The bigger casinos usually have a **race and sports book**, a room where major sports events are televised. Players can bet on just about any game, boxing match or horse race in the country, except for those taking place in Nevada. Race and sports books are best during major events, when everyone is captivated by, betting on and yelling about the same thing.

Las Vegas literally has scores of casinos, all offering different games and odds. The following pages describe the major players on Las Vegas Blvd, plus a few old-school, partyin' and kitschy gambling-hall faves on and off the Strip. All are always open, don't charge admission, offer free self-service and valet parking (tip at least $2) and are wheelchair-accessible.

CASINO CATCHPHRASES

all in – to bet everything you've got
comps – free perks given to frequent gamblers
cooler – an unlucky gambler who makes everyone else lose
dealertainer – a card dealer with an act (eg impersonating Elvis)
eye in the sky – high-tech casino surveillance systems
fold – to throw in your cards and stop betting
high roller – a big gambler, aka 'whale'
line pass – lets you skip the queue at nightclubs
low roller – a small-time gambler (eg likes penny slot machines)
marker – IOU debt owed to a casino
one-armed bandit – old-fashioned nickname for a slot machine
pit boss – the casino card dealers' manager
sucker bet – a gamble on nearly impossible odds
toke – a tip or gratuity
trips – three of a kind

GAMBLING & CASINOS

BELLAGIO

Inspired by the beauty of the lakeside Italian village, and irreverently built by Steve Wynn on the site of the legendary Dunes, the **Bellagio** (Map p182; ☎ 693-7111; www.bellagio.com; 3600 Las Vegas Blvd S; Ⓜ Bally's & Paris) is Vegas' original opulent, if entirely parvenu, pleasure palazzo. The hoi polloi's view from the Strip is of an artificial lake – a veritable oasis in the desert – from which spring a thousand dancing fountains (p71). At the water's edge is a cluster of butter-yellow Tuscan buildings perpetrating the illusion of having being plucked from Italy's Lake District.

Although the nouveau-riche stink can be heady, the secret delight of the Bellagio is that romance is always in the air, and natural light swathes plenty of private nooks. Beyond the glass-and-metal porte cochere you'll find a stable of world-class restaurants (p92), a swish shopping concourse (p81), a fine-art gallery (p67) and a European-style casino.

The hotel's gasp-worthy lobby is blowsily adorned with a backlit glass sculpture composed of 2000 hand-blown flowers in vibrant colors. Real flowers, cultivated in a gigantic on-site greenhouse, brighten countless vases throughout the property and an immodestly over-the-top conservatory (p72). In the courtyard, the swimming pool is ensconced by private cabañas and accented by artfully formed citrus and parterre-style gardens. A luxury spa tower and hot nightlife are the lavish icing atop this slightly stale five-diamond cake.

Baby strollers and unaccompanied children under 18 are not allowed at the Bellagio.

Circo (p92), Bellagio

CAESARS PALACE

Vegas' first fully realized megaresort, **Caesars Palace** (Map p182; ☎ 731-7110; www.caesarspalace.com; 3570 Las Vegas Blvd S; Ⓜ Flamingo/Caesars Palace) upped the luxury ante for the gaming industry when it debuted in the heady 1960s. The Greco-Roman fantasyland captured the world's attention with its full-size marble reproductions of classical statuary, its Stripside row of towering fountains and its cocktail waitresses costumed as goddesses.

Thanks to ongoing megabucks renovations, Caesars is redefining its swanky self. Most recently the sybaritic Garden of the Gods Oasis pool complex appeared, where goddesses proffer frozen grapes in summer, and topless sunbathing is allowed at the Venus pool. Inside, neon and cheesy mirrors were replaced with hand-painted murals.

Despite the upgrades, the Palace remains quintessentially kitschy Vegas. Bar girls continue to roam the gaming areas in skimpy togas, and the fountains are still out front – the same ones daredevil Evil Knievel made famous when he jumped them on a motorcycle on December 31, 1967.

Two imperial casinos contain 100 card tables and a couple of thousand slots that will accept up to $500 chips, as well as a state-of-the-art race and sports book with giant TV screens. Fashionistas saunter inside the upscale Forum Shops (p20), bizarrely featuring an aquarium and animatronic fountain shows, as well as a permanent exhibition of exotic cars (p85). The Colosseum, a 4000-seat showroom modeled after its Roman namesake, was custom built for lavish, if severely overpriced, theatrical spectacles.

Caesars appears poised to rule the empire once again.

Caesars Palace

GAMBLING & CASINOS

MGM GRAND

With over 5000 rooms, the $1-billion **MGM Grand** (Map p182; ☎ 891-7777; www
.mgmgrand.com; 3799 Las Vegas Blvd S; Ⓜ MGM Grand) retains the 'world's largest
hotel' crown, despite mounting competition from the Genting Highlands
resort complex in Kuala Lumpur. The MGM contains no less than 18,000
doors, 7778 beds and 93 elevators. And we could keep overwhelming you
with trivial statistics all day long. But the important thing is that despite its
enormous size, the shimmering emerald-green 'City of Entertainment' –
which appears like something straight out of *The Wizard of Oz* – has done
an amazing job of making its *au courant* scene seem intimate, even clubby.

Owned by movie mogul Metro Goldwyn Mayer, the MGM has co-opted
themes from Hollywood movies, right down to photos of yesteryear's
film stars hanging in the public bathroom stalls. The casino consists of
one gigantic, circular room with an ornate domed ceiling and replicated
1930s glamor. The gaming area is equal in size to four football fields and
offers a whopping selection of slots and the full spectrum of table games,
plus the requisite race and sports book and a hot poker room.

Out front, it's hard to miss the USA's largest bronze statue, a 100,000lb
(45,360kg) lion that's 45ft (14m) tall, perched atop a pedestal ringed
by fountains, lush landscaping and Atlas-themed statues. The MGM's
'Maximum Vegas' attractions include the lion habitat (p72), the gigantic
Grand Garden Arena that often hosts championship boxing bouts and
megaconcerts, the saucy La Femme topless revue (p137) and an impressive celebrity-chef line-up (p98).

Bronze lion, MGM Grand

Gina Lubrano
High-limit baccarat dealer at the Mansion, MGM Grand (opposite)

How long you've been a dealer Since I was 21 years old. My mother was a dealer, too. **First game you dealt** Everybody starts out dealing blackjack. But you have to start learning different games if you want to move up. **Favorite casino game to deal** Blackjack, because I get to talk to the players. **The secret of a dealer's success** The most difficult thing is the posture a dealer has to take. You can't take anything personally. **Good-luck rituals gamblers use** Many of the Asian players will bring itty-bitty gold Buddhas. Some gamblers never change their clothes. **The best players are** Tippers. **What's changed most about this city** Nobody really gets dressed up in Las Vegas anymore, which is too bad. But by the same token, you can be walking around in a pair of sweats and go just about anyplace. **Don't-miss restaurants for first-time visitors** Mon Ambi Gabi (p102) or the Bellagio's coffee shop.

MIRAGE

There's nothing quite like casino mogul Steve Wynn's most exotic creation, **Mirage** (Map p180; ☎ 791-7111; www.mirage.com; 3400 Las Vegas Blvd S; 🚌 The Deuce), which opened back in 1989. Its paradisiacal tropical setting, replete with an atrium filled with jungle foliage and waterfalls (p72), captures the imagination. Out front in a lagoon, the fiery trademark faux volcano (p71) erupts nightly, inevitably stopping onlookers in their tracks.

Woven into the interior waterscape are scores of bromeliads enveloped in sunlight and fed by a computerized misting system. The airy scents of jasmine and vanilla are often wafting. Circling the atrium is a huge Polynesian-themed casino, which incorporates the unique design concept of placing gaming areas under separate roofs to invoke a feeling of intimacy. Real and faux tropical plants add to the splendor of the casino, which also boasts a popular high-stakes poker room.

But all of that is the old Mirage. The new theme is 'remixed.' Until recently the Mirage had been outstripped by newer, splashier megaresorts, including Steve Wynn's eponymous resort just up the road. But this landmark has climbed back to the top of the Strip game by adding the hot nightclub Jet (p131) and powerhouse eateries (p100) such as Stack, Japonais and the totally re-envisioned Fin.

By the casino's south entrance, a royal white tiger habitat permits a peek at a parade of big cats – if you're lucky, it'll be feeding time. Although the dynamic duo is no longer performing, you can still visit Siegfried & Roy's Secret Garden & Dolphin Habitat (p73), though it makes animal-lovers queasy.

Lounge bar in the Mirage

VENETIAN

Impresario Sheldon Adelson broke ground on his replica of La Repubblica Serenissima ('Most Serene Republic') – reputed to be the home of the world's first casino – shortly after the controversial and dramatic implosion of the vintage Sands casino hotel in 1996. On this hallowed ground the fabulous Rat Pack once gathered. This was where Frank Sinatra, Dean Martin, Sammy Davis Jr and the rest of the gang hobnobbed with movie stars, senators and showgirls. When the Sands came tumbling down, a piece of history was lost – but new royalty was born.

Inspired by the splendor of Italy's most-romantic city, the luxury megaresort **Venetian** (Map p180; ☎ 414-1000; www.venetian.com; 3355 Las Vegas Blvd S; M Harrah's/Imperial Palace) boasts reproductions of Venetian landmarks including the doge's palace, *campanile* (bell tower), St Mark's Sq and even a mini Rialto Bridge with a historical escalator added. Graceful bridges, flowing canals, vibrant piazzas and welcoming stone walkways faithfully imitate the Venetian spirit, especially inside the Grand Canal Shoppes (p80) where gondolas (p70) set sail.

The newest addition is the all-suite Venezia Tower, with its exclusive concierge level. Other amenities include sultry Tao (p132) nightclub; the stunning Guggenheim Hermitage Museum (p67), which has a hidden homage to Michelangelo's Sistine Chapel; the world-class Canyon Ranch SpaClub (p124) and fitness center; and top-drawer gourmet restaurants (p105), some with star chefs confidently at the helm.

The swanky casino is linked to the ever-expanding, state-of-the-art Sands Expo convention center.

Gondola ride inside the Venetian

WYNN

Instead of an exploding volcano or an Eiffel tower out front to lure the crowds, legend Steve Wynn's eponymous resort **Wynn** (Map p180; ☎ 770-7000; www.wynnlasvegas.com; 3145 Las Vegas Blvd S; 🚍 The Deuce) is all about exclusivity – getting inside is the goal, so that you can then scoff at the hoi polloi flooding Las Vegas Blvd, secure in your lavish retreat. Reserve a suite and you'll even get to use a private VIP side entrance.

Perhaps the most remarkable thing about Wynn is the painstaking attention paid to detail. In fact, it's as if the Mirage and Bellagio were only Wynn's rough drafts. Elements of both of the mogul's former projects peek through here. It sports the decor of the Bellagio, but with more vibrant colors and inlaid flower mosaics. Lush greenery recalls the Mirage, but with panoramic windows, natural light and outdoor seating at every turn.

The signature (literally – it has Wynn's name written in script across the top, punctuated by an emphatic period) copper-toned hotel is shielded from the Strip by an artificial 'mountain.' Slack-jawed tourists cross over footbridges into the resort, waltzing by the haute-couture shops and the Ferrari-Maserati dealership of Wynn Esplanade (p82) and past a stable of five-star restaurants (p106). Inside the enormous casino is a popular poker room that's attracting pros around the clock; slot machines from a penny up to $5K per pull; a cavernous race and sports book; and a spread of high-minimum table games, along with poolside blackjack for guests.

Wynn plans to operate a free shuttle service to and from the monorail.

BEST BETS FOR DIEHARD PLAYERS

> Blackjack – table rules vary, but check out North Strip casinos like the Sahara or downtown's Vegas Club and El Cortez
> Craps – the odds may change; good times roll at the Strip's Casino Royale, downtown's Main Street Station and off-Strip Sam's Town
> Race and sports books – the Hilton has the world's largest, while Bally's downstairs is for quick-and-dirty bets; downtown's Vegas Club has prize-worthy sports memorabilia
> Roulette – Paris-Las Vegas has the USA's only authentic wheel – for high rollers
> Video poker – the Palms and Hilton have full-pay machines, while the vintage El Cortez is best for nickel-and-dime players

BINION'S

The Horseshoe was opened in 1951 by notorious Texan gambler Benny Binion, who sported gold coins for buttons on his tailored cowboy shirts. It was Binion who oversaw the transformation of downtown's Fremont St from a row of sawdust gambling halls into 'Glitter Gulch' with its classy carpet joints giving away free drinks to slot-machine players and sending limos to the airport for high-rollin' whales. In the grand Las Vegas tradition of one-upmanship, **Binion's** (Map pp184-5; ☎ 382-1600, 800-937-6537; www.binions.com; 128 E Fremont St; 🚍 The Deuce) once offered punters a chance to drool over $1 million worth of gold certificates kept in a glass display case shaped, appropriately enough, like a lucky horseshoe.

A savvy horse trader, Binion once quipped 'An honest deal makes its own friends,' and his casino became best known for its 'zero limit' betting policy and as the place where the World Series of Poker began. These are just some of the reasons why the tables are filled day and night. Another is Binion's larger-than-life standing among Strip casino giants, despite being a diminutive downtown gambling hall. Now that Benny's gone to the great round-up in the sky, his namesake casino is struggling to live up to its legacy. But it's still worth hitting this country-and-western flavored casino, if only to swing by the high-stakes poker room at the back to witness nail-biting, around-the-clock Texas Hold'em action.

If you win big, you can pay your respects to Benny's statue, at the northeast corner of Ogden Ave and Casino Center Blvd, before galloping out of downtown.

No 1 reason to come to Binion's...

FLAMINGO

In 1946 the **Flamingo** (Map p182; ☎ 733-3111; www.flamingolv.com; 3555 Las Vegas Blvd S; Ⓜ Flamingo/Caesars Palace) was the talk of the town. Its original owners – all members of the New York mafia – shelled out millions to build this tropical gaming oasis in the desert. Billy Wilkerson, owner of the *Hollywood Reporter* and a string of sizzling-hot LA nightclubs, broke ground here. The industry insider had grand visions of recreating the Sunset Strip in the Silver State. But he ran out of money fast, so the mob stepped in.

It was prime gangster Americana, initially managed by the infamous mobster Ben 'Bugsy' Siegel, who named it after his girlfriend, a dancer named Virginia Hill called 'The Flamingo' for her red hair and long legs. Siegel died in a hail of bullets at Hill's Beverly Hills home soon after the Flamingo opened, the victim of a contract killing. The Flamingo had gotten off to a slow start and the investors believed the Flamingo would fail, so they 'took care of business.' They made a whopping mistake: not only did the Flamingo survive, but it has continued to thrive.

Today, the Flamingo isn't quite what it was back when its janitorial staff wore tuxedos; think more *Miami Vice*, less *Bugsy*. But it's always manically crowded in the casino, where there are some low-limit tables and slots, plus free gambling lessons. Drop by during the madhouse happy hour to sling back heavy-hitting margaritas out of fab souvenir glasses and watch women of questionable repute stroll by the glitzy revolving doors – Bugsy would've been proud.

Keeping with the theme, the Flamingo

LUXOR

Named after Egypt's splendid ancient city, the landmark **Luxor** (Map p182; ☎ 262-4444; www.luxor.com; Luxor, 3900 Las Vegas Blvd S; 🚌 The Deuce) has the biggest 'wow!' factor of the South Strip's megaresorts. It tenuously hangs in the balance between being a pyramid of gaudiness and a refined shrine to Egyptian art, architecture and antiquities.

Fronting the signature 30-story pyramid cloaked in black glass from base to apex is a crouching sphinx and a sandstone obelisk etched with hieroglyphics. The pyramid's interior is stuffed full of enormous Egyptian statues of guards, lions and rams; grand sandstone columns and walls adorned with tapestries; a stunning replica of the Great Temple of Ramses II; and a pharaoh's treasure of polished marble.

A renowned Egyptologist oversaw the production of the King Tut Museum (p67) pieces, which may be hard to appreciate without snickering due to the odd casino setting. On exhibit are replicas of King Tut's innermost gold-leaf coffin, decorated with thousands of simulated precious stones; an antechamber furnished with wooden and gold funerary beds carved in the form of animals; and a treasury containing miniature wooden boats intended to carry Tutankhamen on his voyage to the afterworld. The facsimile of wealth on display will make you hunger even more to hit that slot-machine jackpot.

High above the ho-hum casino in the Pharaoh's Pavilion, thrills and chills await at the revved-up Games of the Gods arcade, complete with virtual-reality rides; an IMAX cinema (p141) and motion-simulator ride films; and the multisensory Pirates 4D adventure.

The Great Sphinx, Luxor

MANDALAY BAY

The vaguely tropically themed **'M-Bay'** (Map p182; ☎ 632-7777; www.mandalay bay.com; 3950 Las Vegas Blvd S; 🚌 The Deuce) fails to match the grandeur of Vegas' more famous megaresorts, although high-stakes gamblers will appreciate a classy casino that seems as limitless as the credit line needed to play here. The resort pushed its star-studded strategy by inviting legendary tenor Luciano Pavarotti to sing at the gala opening of the Events Center, which hosts championship boxing matches, and by adding a House of Blues entertainment complex (p126), topped by the exclusive VIP-only Foundation Room (p131).

Everything can be a spectacle here, if you know where to look. There's rock-star karaoke at the House of Blues (see the boxed text, p139), after-dark aerial acrobatics at rumjungle (see the boxed text, p121), catsuit-clad 'angels' scaling the wine tower at Aureole (p96), and a frozen vodka locker where sable fur coats are lent to members at Red Square (see the boxed text, p121). Stylish boutique extras include Mandalay Place (p81), a skybridge shopping promenade, and the minimalist modern THEhotel with its lofty Mix bar (p129) and chic bathhouse spa (p123).

M-Bay's aquatic theme hinges on the Shark Reef (p73), an awesome glassed-in aquarium, and artificial Mandalay Beach, built with 1700 tons of imported California sand and featuring summer surfing competitions, starlight concerts and the clothing-optional Moorea Beach Club. If the stress of gambling at the high-minimum tables gets to be too much, you can also float away on a lazy river ride.

Free trams shuttle between Mandalay Bay and the Luxor and Excalibur resorts.

rumjungle (p121), Mandalay Bay

NEW YORK-NEW YORK

Give me your tired, huddled (over a Wheel of Fortune slot machine) masses. The mini-megapolis of **New York-New York** (Map p182; ☎ 740-6969; www.nynyhotelcasino.com; 3790 Las Vegas Blvd S; M MGM Grand) features scaled-down replicas of the towering Empire State Building and Statue of Liberty, a mini Brooklyn Bridge and scale-warped renditions of the Chrysler, Ziggurat and Liberty Plaza buildings, all topped off by a Coney Island–style roller coaster (p69) wrapped around the flashy facade. The crowd is young and party-hardy.

Zany design elements throughout reflect NYC's bold color, history and diversity. The attention to detail is incredible, with whiffs of steam rising from faux manhole covers near the elevators. Don't overlook the ornate Rockefeller restrooms or the playful USA bas-relief map at America coffee shop. Claustrophobes, beware: this Disneyfied version of the Big Apple can get even more crowded than the real deal: around 200,000 pedestrians stride across NYC's Brooklyn Bridge each year, but an estimated 15 million traverse the Vegas version on an annual basis.

Clews of slots and gaming tables are set against a rich backdrop of famous landmarks, with high-limit Gaming on the Green. Cloaked in red velvet, the gorgeous Big Apple Bar dominates the casino, with an elevated stage where hot lounge acts belt it out. The Bar at Times Square is famous for its dueling piano acts, but you can sip a more civilized pint outdoors at Nine Fine Irishmen, where live Celtic bands play. Sports fans gravitate to ESPN Zone (p120), which has a high-tech arcade upstairs (p69).

Manhattan Express (p69), New York-New York

PARIS-LAS VEGAS

Adorned with fake Francophonic signs like 'Le Buffet' and 'Le Sports Book,' the multimillion-dollar Gallic caricature **Paris-Las Vegas** (Map p182; ☎ 946-7000; www.parislasvegas.com; 3655 Las Vegas Blvd S; Ⓜ Bally's & Paris) strives to evoke the gaiety of the grand dame by re-creating her most famous landmarks, including the Paris Opera House, Arc de Triomphe, Hotel de Ville, Louvre and even the River Seine, which frames the property. Just like in the French capital, the signature attraction at this place is the ersatz Eiffel Tower (p68), where visitors can ascend in a glass elevator to dine romantically on modern French cuisine at tables overlooking the Strip (p102).

Surrounded by street scenes from both banks of the Seine, the bustling vault-ceilinged casino complete with replica Métropolitain arches is home to almost a hundred gaming tables, a couple of thousand slot machines, a popular race and sports book and the USA's only authentic French roulette wheel (it has no '0' or '00') in the high-limit area. Crème de la crème champagne is waiting on ice at Napoleon's bar (p121) or you can wear what you eat by indulging in a caviar facial at the Spa by Mandara (p125).

Paris is conveniently connected to Bally's monorail station by a petit shopping arcade, Le Boulevard, where high heels clack along cobblestone streets.

Outside Paris-Las Vegas

SAHARA

Standing in the no-man's-land of the North Strip, where old-school casinos are being demolished with the speed of a freight train, the **Sahara** (Map p180; ☎ 737-2111; www.saharavegas.com; 2535 Las Vegas Blvd S; Ⓜ Sahara) is a real survivor. Thanks to a $100-million face-lift, the Moroccan-themed casino is one of the few vintage Vegas carpet joints to withstand the onslaught of corporate megaresorts. Since the Sahara first threw open its doors in 1952, its Conga Room showcased everyone from jazz virtuoso Ella Fitzgerald to the Beatles. Elvis Presley and Elizabeth Taylor once lounged by the swimming pool adorned with Moroccan mosaic tiles and private cabañas.

The Arabian-nights theme continues inside the casino, with its gold-painted ceilings, molded columns laced with colorful vines and over two dozen golden chandeliers guarded by severe-looking statues of Middle Eastern sultans. The casino also hustles the Strip's largest variety of unique card games, including some you've never heard of (and thus will quickly lose all of your dough at). Stick to the low-minimum blackjack tables with good odds.

These days the Sahara is quite a bit less glamorous than it sounds. Its bread-and-butter crowd is Nascar racing fans, who knock back bottles of Bud in the Nascar Café, where the centerpiece is the monstrous Carzilla, the world's largest stock car, designed by Dale Earnhardt. More compelling for speed freaks are the thrill rides, especially a rollercoaster that reaches a top speed of 70mph as it loops from underground through the Sahara's camel marquee sign and up a 200ft (61m) tower (p69).

Speed – the Ride, Sahara

GAMBLING & CASINOS

STRATOSPHERE

Las Vegas has many buildings exceeding 20 stories, but only the **Stratosphere** (Map p180; ☎ 380-7777; www.stratospherehotel.com; 2000 Las Vegas Blvd S; Ⓜ Sahara) tops a hundred. At 1149ft (350m), the three-legged, $550-million Stratosphere Tower is the tallest building in the USA west of the Mississippi River. At the base of the tapered tower is a casino that has all the glorious trappings of a redneck patriot's trailer park, but little in the way of a theme (although it does boast low-limit table games and 1500 reputedly loose slots and video poker machines).

Atop the Strip's lucky landmark are indoor and outdoor viewing decks, which afford the city's best 360-degree panoramas. You will also find a revolving restaurant (p103) and lounge (p129) up here. To get you there, the tower boasts America's fastest elevators; they ascend and descend at over 20mph, lifting you 108 floors in a mere 37 ear-popping seconds. But we didn't need to tell you this because the attendants will chatter away at you, dispensing trivia during the whole ride. Once you have sufficiently recovered, you can attack the tower's high-altitude thrill rides (p70).

Back down inside the low-roller's casino, you can stuff your face with comfort food while being serenaded by the swingin' waitstaff at Roxy's Diner (p103), then spend the rest of your chump change in the nearby kingdom of kitsch, Bonanza Gifts (p88), or on tickets to one of the Strip's cheesiest production shows like the laughably bad late-night vampire girlie show *Bite*.

Outside Stratosphere

TI (TREASURE ISLAND)

Yo, ho, whoa: the shift at **TI** (Map p180; ☎ 894-7111; www.treasureisland.com; 3300 Las Vegas Blvd S; 🚌 The Deuce) from family-friendly to bawdy and oh so naughty epitomizes Vegas' racy efforts to put 'sin' back in 'casino.' Though traces of Treasure Island's original swashbuckling skull-and-crossbones theme linger (if you look hard), this tonier, terra-cotta–toned resort strives to re-create an elegant Caribbean hideaway. It practically screams 'leave the kids at home.' And it prefers to be known only by its initials now, thank you very much. Just like J-Lo and K-Fed, ya know?

You'll approach the property via a wood-bottomed, hemp-roped bridge that spans the artificial Sirens' Cove, set beside a vague replica of an 18th-century sea village. The spicy Sirens of TI's (p72) ships – a Spanish privateer vessel and a British frigate – face off several times nightly, manned by femme-fatale pirates dressed like lingerie models. The adults-only theme continues inside the sprawling casino. One-armed Playboy bandits await where plastic chests full-o-booty once reigned. The slot machines and gaming tables are tightly grouped, but no one seems to mind – the place is always packed.

The casino hotel's latest grown-up additions are deluxe poolside cabañas, a huge party-friendly hot tub, the Stripside burlesque lounge and nightclub Tangerine (p130) and tequila goddesses at Isla Mexican Kitchen (p104). Easing the journey here and back again is a free tram to and from the Mirage next door. So now you've got a handy alibi when stopping by for a quick squeeze – of the slot-machine handles, of course.

Sirens of TI (p72)

GAMBLING & CASINOS

OTHER CASINOS

BALLY'S Map p182

☎ 967-4111; www.ballyslasvegas.com; 3645 Las Vegas Blvd S; Ⓜ Bally's & Paris

Unless it's 'bigger is better,' there's no real theme at the Strip's most staid megaresort, with a football field–sized casino overhung by twinkling chandeliers and velvet-lined chairs. But Bally's biggest attractions are non-gaming. Sunday's epic Sterling Brunch (p92) has French champagne and cracked crab legs galore. *Jubilee!* (p137) is one of Vegas' long-running showgirl extravaganzas, and after performances the leggy dancers often pose for their over-the-hill admirers at the casino's Indigo lounge.

CALIFORNIA Map pp184-5

☎ 385-1222; www.thecal.com; 12 E Ogden Ave; 🚌 The Deuce

At many Vegas casinos, a lucky spin of a slot machine will earn you a brand-spanking new BMW, a racy Jaguar or a red-hot convertible. At the downtown 'just-call-me-Cal' California, one very lucky nickel-slots player will someday ride home in a – drum roll please – a brand-new PT Cruiser! That simple fact tells you a lot about the 1970s-era Cal, 'the hotel with aloha spirit,' where even the dealers wear Hawaiian shirts. Incidentally, over 80% of the Cal's guests hail

from the 50th state. A skybridge connects to Main Street Station.

CIRCUS CIRCUS Map p180

☎ 734-0410; www.circuscircus.com; 2880 Las Vegas Blvd S; 🚌 The Deuce

While cruising the bedraggled North Strip, it's pretty hard to miss the 1968 vintage Circus Circus, what with its enormous clown-shaped marquee and tent-shaped casino under a gaudily striped big top. From the outside, this sprawling resort may look pretty cheesy – and it definitely *is*. It's also overrun with kiddies and baby strollers. If you're a real wild child, you can relive scenes from Hunter S Thompson's *Fear and Loathing in Las Vegas*, but even without the drugs, it's hallucinogenic enough. Above the casino floor, trapeze artists, high-wire workers, jugglers and unicyclists perform stunts (p70), while out back lies the Adventuredome (p68). Cacophonous Slots-A-Fun (p76) is just a drunken stumble away.

EL CORTEZ Map pp184-5

☎ 385-5200; www.elcortezhotelcasino .com; 600 E Fremont St; 🚌 The Deuce

A classic dive dating back to 1940, El Cortez is choked with smoke but has vintage Vegas appeal in spades. In the crowded casino, rough-edged local gamblers grudgingly allow accidental tourists like yourself to buy into the low-limit action on roulette, craps and other table games aimed at cheapskates and gambling novices. El Cortez is the kind of place where it's almost impossible to lose your shirt, but you'll need a few stiff drinks first. It's a few blocks east of the Fremont Street Experience, which may make some nervous. Then again, if that kind of thing bothered you, you wouldn't even be thinking of visiting this seriously seedy place.

⊙ EXCALIBUR Map p182

☎ 597-7777; www.excalibur.com; 3850 Las Vegas Blvd S; Ⓜ MGM Grand
Arthurian legends aside, this medieval caricature with a faux drawbridge epitomizes gaudy Vegas. Excalibur could have resembled an elegant English castle, but its designers decided to go the kitschy route, which is just fine with the cheapo families with rambunctious young kids who stay here. Inside the castle, the casino walls are hung with coats of arms and cheap stained-glass art of valiant knights. Down on the Fantasy Faire Midway are buried Ye Olde carnival games like skee-ball, with joystick joys and Merlin's Magic Motion Machine film rides in the Wizard's Arcade. For kids, the Tournament of Kings dinner show is a demolition derby with hooves and sticky fingers.

⊙ GOLDEN GATE Map pp184-5

☎ 385-1906; www.goldengatecasino.net; 1 E Fremont St; Ⓑ The Deuce
This old-fashioned gambling hall and hotel has stood on the corner of Fremont and Main Sts since 1906, one year after this whistle-stop railway town was founded. It transformed into the Golden Gate in the 1950s, when a troupe of Italian-Americans from San Francisco decamped at what was once known as the 'Sal Sagev' (the city's name spelled backward, doncha know). Today the Golden Gate's hypnotic mechanical sign is almost as irresistible as its famous 99¢ shrimp cocktails (p109), over 25 million parfait-glasses of which have already been sold. The snug casino boasts lively craps tables and double-deck blackjack being dealt to the nostalgic sounds of live piano music.

BEST LOW-ROLLER CASINOS

Whether you're looking for nickel video-poker machines or roulette wheels with 25¢ minimum bets, you can bravely start slumming downtown at El Cortez (p54), Golden Gate (p55), Plaza (p58) or Vegas Club (p61) and on the Strip at the Stratosphere (p52) and loud-as-hell **Casino Royale** (☎ 800-854-7666; www.casinoroyalehotel.com; 3411 Las Vegas Blvd S).

🔵 GOLDEN NUGGET Map pp184-5
☎ 385-7111; www.goldennugget.com;
129 E Fremont St; 🚌 **The Deuce**

The Golden Nugget's claim to fame was once the Hand of Faith, the heftiest hunk of gold ever found, weighing a massive 61lb 11oz (28kg). But that's not all this bejeweled casino is known for. When it debuted as the world's largest casino in 1946, the Nugget looked like a million bucks and poker players were allowed to deal their own cards. In the 1970s, casino impresario Steve Wynn made vintage Vegas cool again by inviting Frank Sinatra to star at the Theatre Ballroom. The enterprising 21st-century wunderkind duo Tim Poster and Thomas Breitling catapulted the Nugget into the national limelight on the reality TV series *Casino*. Nowadays the glittering casino has a spread of table games, notably a cool poker room, but the crowd is the antithesis of hip.

🔵 HARD ROCK Map pp190-1
☎ 800-473-7625; www.hardrockhotel .com; **4455 Paradise Rd;** 🚌 **108, 202**

The hot, hot, hot hotel that defines Vegas hip opens onto a roomy circular casino with a state-of-the-art race and sports book. Raised above the main casino floor are The Joint rock-concert venue (p126), Body English nightclub (p130), ultratrendy restaurants (p112 and p113) and a priceless handful of boutique

The Joint (p126), Hard Rock

shops (p80). There's seasonal swim-up blackjack at the Beach Club, open to the public on Rehab Sundays (see the boxed text, p123). All in all, this sexy, see-and-be-seen scene is perfect for entourage wannabes.

HOOTERS Map p182
☎ 866-584-6687; www.hooterscasino hotel.com; 115 E Tropicana Ave; 🚌 202

With a slapdash, thrown-together atmosphere, the ex–San Remo casino hotel comes off feeling exactly like your pervy next-door-neighbor's rec room circa, oh, 1970. Although the Hooters girls look loose, the slots definitely are not – and neither are the rules for sitting down at the crowded tables games. That's the price you have to pay for the privilege of ogling Hooters girls in tight T-shirts all night long as you happily lose your own shirt gambling here.

IMPERIAL PALACE Map p180
☎ 731-3311; www.imperialpalace.com; 3535 Las Vegas Blvd S; Ⓜ Harrah's/ Imperial Palace

The blue-roofed pagoda facade and faux–Far East theme are hokey, but the zany atmosphere at what was once the Flamingo Capri is quite alright. If you liked the indie movie *The Cooler*, you'll love it here. Time your visit to coincide with the evening shift change of the 'dealertainers'

(p75), celebrity impersonators who do double duty as dealers. Lots of low-minimum table games to be found here.

MONTE CARLO Map p182
☎ 730-7777; www.montecarlo.com; 3770 Las Vegas Blvd S; 🚌 The Deuce

Fronted by Corinthian colon-nades, triumphal arches, petite dancing fountains and allegorical statuary, this glittering casino is bustling and spacious. A magnificent marble-floored, crystal-chandeliered lobby with Palladian windows is reminiscent of a European grand hotel, but otherwise this is a poor person's Bellagio rather than an evocation of the grandeur of its namesake in Monaco. For entertainment, there's master magician Lance Burton (p139), many critics' pick for Vegas' best illusionist. Other reasons for stopping by are classy Houdini's Lounge and the sporty Monte Carlo Pub & Brewery (p101).

ORLEANS Map pp188-9
☎ 365-7111; www.orleanscasino.com; 4500 W Tropicana Ave; 🚌 201

A mile west of the Strip, this New Orleans–themed casino hotel has done a so-so job of re-creating the Big Easy. Among its most popular diversions are the 70-lane bowling alley, 18-screen cineplex and specialty bars like Brendan's Irish Pub (p125), which has live

GAMBLING & CASINOS

music. Entertainment legends such as Willie Nelson and LeAnn Rimes have performed in the Orleans showroom, while megaconcerts and sports events take place in the arena out back. The high-ceilinged casino is an airy, rectangular room; on the floor are more than 3000 slot, video poker and video keno machines, plus $5-minimum card tables and a 39-table poker room with twice-daily tournaments.

PALMS Map pp188-9
☎ 866-942-7777; www.palms.com; 4321 W Flamingo Rd; 🚌 202

The ultra-modern Palms casino hotel offers eclectic entertainment designed to seduce gen-Xers and gen-Yers. It jumped into the limelight with a starring role on MTV's 'Real World' reality TV series and Bravo's 'Celebrity Poker Showdown.' The high-drama, neon-lit atmosphere is equal parts sexy and downright sleazy – you'll have to pay just to take a look inside the new Playboy Club atop the Fantasy Tower. The main casino has quick cocktail service and a heavenly spread of full-pay video poker machines, plus two poker rooms. The first-rate multiplex hosts the CineVegas film festival (p127). Other places to see and be seen include leather-clad Hart & Huntington Tattoo Shop, ghostbar (p128), N9NE steakhouse (p115) and towering Alizé (p113).

PLANET HOLLYWOOD
Map p182
☎ 785-5555; www.planethollywood .com; 3667 Las Vegas Blvd S; Ⓜ Bally's & Paris

Dating from the 1950s, the original Aladdin, where Elvis and Priscilla Presley tied the knot, was dramatically imploded in 1998. Retooled to target the Asian and European jet-set, the new Aladdin megaresort threw open its doors in 2000. Quickly thereafter the owners made the largest bankruptcy filing ever in Nevada history. By the time you read this, it is quite possible that Planet Hollywood, the Aladdin's new new owners, will finally have dramatically changed this megaresort, which has been losing money almost from the day it opened. But don't hold your breath: no one has ever made a mint with this hexed property – not yet, anyway. Your best bet is shopping at the adjacent Miracle Mile Shops (p81), formerly Desert Passage.

PLAZA Map pp184-5
☎ 386-2110; www.plazahotelcasino .com; 1 Main St; 🚌 The Deuce

Built on the site of the old Union Pacific Railroad Depot, Jackie Gaughan's Plaza is a 1970s time capsule. Like most downtown joints, the Plaza is for hardcore gamblers. Its tacky decor doesn't correspond to any known theme, unless the theme is cheap. Even the chandeliers – yes, there are chandeliers – look gaudy. And that's just fine with the Plaza's patrons, who are hypnotized by the penny slots, nickel video-poker machines and $1 blackjack tables with friendly dealers. The down-and-out Plaza is perennially popular with package tourists and feisty blue-haired ladies who play for keeps in the 400-seat bingo room. Also upstairs is the glass-domed Center Stage bar, which has cockpit views of the Fremont Street Experience.

🎯 RED ROCK
☎ 797-7777; www.redrocklasvegas.com; 11011 W Charleston Blvd, at I-215; 🚌 208

Despite being crammed full of suburbanites, Red Rock is the only off-Strip chain casino to have catapulted itself onto the celebrity A-list, even if only temporarily. Poised within easy striking distance of the southwestern beauty of Red Rock Canyon (p146), this high-concept, high-design casino resort is banking not only on its vast casino, but also on its nouveau spa (p124) and above-average dining and nightlife, from authentic Austin-based Salt Lick BBQ (p115) to Cherry nightclub, designed by Rande Gerber (aka Mr Cindy Crawford). Svelte rooms come with extras like plasma TVs and stereos with iPod docking stations.

Onyx Bar, Red Rock

🎰 RIO Map pp188-9

☎ 800-752-9746; www.playrio.com;
3700 W Flamingo Rd; 🚌 free Strip
shuttle from Harrah's

The name of this wildly popular casino hotel says a lot about the all-suites Rio. The corny Masquerade Village, the center of the action, offers an ongoing *carnaval* atmosphere. In the free 'Show in the Sky,' Mardi Gras floats suspended from tracks in the ceiling parade above the gaming tables while costumed performers dance and lip-synch to jazzy songs. The fun is infectious, and you can ride along in one of the floats and have a souvenir photo taken. In a huge, 100,000-sq-ft (9290-sq-m) casino decked out with a colorful Brazilian motif, 'bevertainers' bring around drinks in between doing song-and-dance numbers. Ringed around the casino are two of the best buffets in town (p114).

🎰 SAM'S TOWN

☎ 456-7777; www.samstownlv.com;
5111 Boulder Hwy, at E Flamingo Rd;
🚌 107, 202

It's such a landmark on the local Vegas scene, The Killers even named their latest album after it. Ranchers, cowboys and RVers flock here, and there's a helluva lot of good stuff to keep 'em all amused. It's a rip-roarin' place to get your feet wet on table games, including some single-deck blackjack. Or you can just peruse

the country-and-western outfitter Sheplers, go bowling and take in a flick at the multiplex cinema, or feed your most gluttonous urges at Billy Bob's Steak House and Saloon, which serves a foot-long Grand Canyon chocolate cake.

🎰 SILVERTON

☎ 263-7777; www.silvertoncasino.com;
3333 Blue Diamond Rd, off I-15; 🚌 117

Built for the same redneck crowd as the Bass Pro Shops Outdoor World next door, the large lodge-style rooms at this conservative casino resort feature the same beds found at the Bellagio, but for a fraction of the price. That way you can afford all of those jelly-beans in your minibar. Or you can keep plugging away nickels and quarters into all of those video-poker and slot machines, just like the retirees who are camped at the RV park out back. Don't miss the coin-op miniature bowling inside an Airstream trailer in Hootie & the Blowfish's Shady Grove Lounge.

🎰 TROPICANA Map p182

☎ 739-2222; www.tropicanalv.com;
3801 Las Vegas Blvd S; Ⓜ MGM Grand

Built in 1957, the Trop has had nearly half a century to sully its shine, lose its crowds and go the way of the Dunes and the Sands – ashes to ashes, dust to dust. But thanks to a few lifts and tucks, it just keeps hanging in there. There's still a festive Polynesian village feel to it all, although the tropical-paradise theme virtually disappears in the casino, except for some faded floral carpets. Entertaining options include the long-running Folies Bergére (p137) and yuk-yuks at the Comedy Stop (p139). Smoke a stogie at the Havana Hideaway before you slip out the door.

☀ **VEGAS CLUB** Map pp184-5
☎ 385-1664; www.vegasclubcasino.net;
18 E Fremont St; 🚌 The Deuce
A sports-themed casino hotel with a Hawaiian twist, the super-duper friendly Vegas Club is noteworthy for its collections of sports memorabilia, such as World Series autographed baseball bats. Naturally there's a race and sports book inside the low-key casino, where dealers don baseball-style uniforms. Be sure to keep an eye out for full-pay video-poker machines and double-deck blackjack table games. Gigantic 9lb (4kg) burgers are served upstairs at the Upper Deck restaurant, or you can get a taste of the islands downstairs at Mahalo Express (p109).

>SEE | SHOP | EAT | PLAY

>1 See 65
>2 Shop 79
>3 Eat 91
>4 Play 119

THE MIRAGE
CASINO & RESORT

DANNY
GANS
ENTERTAINER
OF THE YEAR

CAESARS
PALACE
CELINE
DION

On the streets of Las Vegas

👁 SEE

Baby, there's no shortage of things to see in Las Vegas. In fact, the one sure bet in this gambling-hall town is that you absolutely won't have time to see or do it all. The city itself is inexhaustible (and that's the way we like it!).

That goes double for the Strip, where the vast majority of casino hotels are standing and where the array of free to stratospherically priced attractions both day and night can be head spinning. You could spend all day in just one of the Strip's famous megaresorts, and still not experience everything it has to offer.

When you grow weary of all that glitz on the Strip, it's worth checking out the vintage vibe downtown, the hipster arts scene in the Naked City, offbeat museums and more in Vegas' outlying neighborhoods and any of the grand natural diversions lying just outside the city limits (p143).

As you ambitiously sketch out your day over a breakfast buffet, remember to factor in the substantial time it takes to get around the Las Vegas metro area, whether for quickie trips along the Strip or when driving all the way out to the 'burbs and beyond.

WELCOME TO FABULOUS LAS VEGAS

Straddling Las Vegas Blvd south of the Strip is the city's most iconic sign, 'Welcome to Fabulous Las Vegas Nevada.' Cruising by, you might see limos pulled up alongside the road and camera happy tourists dashing out onto the median to get a souvenir photo of themselves by the vintage sign. Of course, when Betty Willis designed it in the late 1950s with an atomic-modern starburst at the top, it wasn't fabulously retro — it was cutting edge hip. Yet it's still 100% pure Vegas, baby.

Top left Cocktail waiter, Flamingo (p46) **Top right** Getting around on two wheels (p162) **Bottom** Cirque du Soleil, Mystère (p138)

MUSEUMS & ART GALLERIES

See also p75 for more unusual and outrageous museums.

ARTS FACTORY Map pp186-7
☎ 676-1111; www.theartsfactory.com; 101-109 E Charleston Blvd; admission free; ☾ most galleries noon-4pm Wed-Sat; ☒ 108; ☐ lot entrance off Boulder Ave

Las Vegas' fractured art scene received an enormous boost in the late '90s. Although photographer Wes Isbutt hadn't set out to establish an art colony in Vegas, that's pretty much what he did. Inside his complex, you'll find hit-and-miss, but always intriguing, contemporary art galleries.

ATOMIC TESTING MUSEUM
Map pp190-1
☎ 794-5161; www.atomictestingmuseum.org; Desert Research Institute, 755 E Flamingo Rd; adult/concession $12/9; ☾ 9am-5pm Mon-Sat, 1-5pm Sun; ☒ 202

During the atomic heyday of the 1950s, gamblers and tourists downtown watched mushroom clouds rising behind downtown's Fremont St, and the city even crowned a Miss Atomic Bomb. Buy your tickets at the replica of a Nevada Test Site guard station outside this awesome 8000-sq-ft (743-sq-m) Smithsonian affiliate. Don't skip seeing the Ground Zero Theater, which mimics a concrete test bunker.

Guggenheim Hermitage Museum, the Venetian

BELLAGIO GALLERY OF FINE ART Map p182

☎ 693-7871, 877-957-9777; www.bellagio.com; Bellagio, 3600 Las Vegas Blvd S; adult/concession $15/12; ⏲ 9am-10pm; Ⓜ Bally's & Paris

Since Steve Wynn sold his baby to MGM Mirage, the Bellagio hasn't been blessed with the same world-class art, but it still hosts blockbuster traveling shows such as *Ansel Adams: America*. Original masterworks also hang inside Picasso restaurant (p93).

COMMERCE STREET STUDIOS Map pp186-7

☎ 678-6278; www.commercestreetstudios.com; 1551 S Commerce St; admission free; 🚌 105

In downtown's Gateway Arts District, these eclectic artists' studios are ground zero for **First Fridays** (www.firstfriday-lasvegas.org), basically giant block parties held on the first Friday evening of every month, with gala gallery openings, live music, street performance art and more.

GUGGENHEIM HERMITAGE MUSEUM Map p180

☎ 414-2440; www.guggenheimlasvegas.org; Venetian, 3355 Las Vegas Blvd S; adult $19, concession $12.50-15; ⏲ 9:30am-7:30pm; Ⓜ Harrah's/Imperial Palace

A partnership with Russia's State Hermitage Museum of St Petersburg ensures the masterpieces keep on coming at this austere gallery designed by Pritzker Prize–winning architect Rem Koolhaas. Look up at the natural skylight, the underside of which flaunts a homage to Michelangelo's Sistine Chapel.

HARD ROCK Map pp190-1

☎ 693-5000; www.hardrockhotel.com; 4455 Paradise Rd; admission free; 🚌 108, 202

The world's first rock'n'roll casino embraces what may be the most impressive collection of rock-star memorabilia ever assembled under one roof. Among the priceless items being watched over by eagle-eyed security guards are some of Elvis' more bodacious fashion statements and Jim Morrison's handwritten lyrics to one of The Doors' greatest hits.

KING TUT MUSEUM Map p182

☎ 262-4000; www.luxor.com; Luxor, 3900 Las Vegas Blvd S; admission $10; ⏲ 10am-11pm; 🚌 The Deuce

Exquisite jeweled reproductions of the artifacts discovered in 1922 by English archaeologist Howard Carter on his descent into the fabled tomb of an obscure Egyptian dynasty are explained during a grandiosely scripted self-guided audio tour.

SEE | SHOP | EAT | PLAY

SEE

◉ LAS VEGAS ART MUSEUM

☎ 360-8000; www.lasvegasartmuseum
.org; 9600 W Sahara Ave; adult $6, concession $3-5; ◷ 10am-5pm Tue-Sat, 1-5pm Sun; 🚌 204

Fans of contemporary art revel in this imposing white edifice filled with light and cutting-edge exhibitions from across the country and abroad. A Smithsonian affiliate, it focuses on the art of the Southwest. The gift shop sells original works.

◉ MAIN STREET STATION

Map pp184-5

☎ 387-1896; www.mainstreetcasino
.com; 200 N Main St; admission free; 🚌 The Deuce

Throughout the neo-Victorian casino are notable *objets d'histoire*, most keeping to the turn-of-the-19th-century theme. Look for an art nouveau chandelier from Paris and stained-glass windows from movie star Lillian Gish's mansion. Strangely, a graffiti-covered chunk of the Berlin Wall now supports the urinals in the men's restroom. Self-guided tour brochures are available at the hotel's front desk.

◉ WYNN COLLECTION Map p180

☎ 770-7000; www.wynnlasvegas.com; Wynn, 3145 Las Vegas Blvd S; admission free; 🚌 The Deuce

Casino mogul Steve Wynn's heavyweight fine-art collection – with original masterpieces by Cézanne, Van Gogh, Matisse, Gauguin, Picasso and Warhol – now graces the walls of his eponymous resort.

◉ THRILL RIDES & AMUSEMENTS

◉ ADVENTUREDOME Map p180

☎ 794-3939; www.adventuredome
.com; Circus Circus, 2880 Las Vegas Blvd S; per ride $4-7, day pass adult/concession $23/15; ◷ call for hours; 🚌 The Deuce

Enclosed by over 8000 pink-glass panes, Circus Circus' indoor amusement park is packed with thrills. Must-rides include the double-loop, double-corkscrew Canyon Blaster and the Sling Shot tower ride packing a whopping four Gs of acceleration. Clowns perform free shows throughout the day.

◉ EIFFEL TOWER EXPERIENCE

Map p182

☎ 946-7000; www.parislasvegas.com; Paris, 3645 Las Vegas Blvd S; adult/concession $9/7; ◷ 9:30am-12:30am, weather permitting; Ⓜ Paris & Bally's

SIZE DOES MATTER

World's biggest hotel MGM Grand
Tallest building in western US Stratosphere Tower
World's largest glass sculpture and tallest chocolate fountain Bellagio
Fastest elevator in the US Stratosphere Tower
World's most powerful beam of light Luxor

How authentic is the half-scale tower? Gustave Eiffel's original drawings were consulted, but the 50-story ersatz replica is welded rather than riveted together. It's also fireproof and engineered to withstand a major earthquake. Ascend in a glass elevator to the observation deck for panoramic views over the Strip, Vegas Valley and mountains.

ESPN ZONE SPORTS ARENA
Map p182

☎ 933-3776; http://espnzone.com/las vegas; New York-New York, 3790 Las Vegas Blvd S; ✷ 11am-10:30pm Mon-Thu, 11am-11:30pm Fri & Sat, 9am-10:30pm Sun; Ⓜ MGM Grand

Venture upstairs from the sports-themed bar and eatery (p120) to play state-of-the-art boxing, pro golfing and other virtual-reality arcade games, go duckpin bowling or scramble up a 30ft (9m) rock-climbing wall.

GAMEWORKS Map p182

☎ 432-4263; www.gameworks.com; 3785 Las Vegas Blvd S; 1/2/3hr unlimited play $20/25/30, all-day pass $35; ✷ 10am-midnight Sun-Thu, 10am-1am Fri & Sat; Ⓜ MGM Grand

Conceived by Steven Spielberg and developed by DreamWorks SKG with Sega and Universal Studios, this high-tech arcade inhabits a large underground space with a full

bar, 75ft (23m) climbing wall ($10), pool tables and loads of multiplayer virtual-reality games. It's only ever crowded – and fun – at night, when entry is restricted to over-21s.

LAS VEGAS CYBER SPEEDWAY & SPEED Map p180

☎ 734-7223; www.nascarcafelasvegas .com; Sahara, 2535 Las Vegas Blvd S; single ride/all-day pass $10/20; ✷ Speedway 10am-midnight Sun-Thu, 10am-1am Fri & Sat, Speed 11am-midnight, 11am-1am Fri & Sat; Ⓜ Sahara

The Speedway's Indy car simulators are so lifelike that they excite real Formula One drivers. The artificial racers are bolted to hydraulic platforms fronting 20ft (7m) wraparound screens that are scary in their realism. Speed, an electromagnetic roller-coaster, slingshots to a top speed of 70mph.

MANHATTAN EXPRESS
Map p182

☎ 740-6969; www.nynyhotelcasino .com; New York-New York, 3790 Las Vegas Blvd S; ride $12.50, re-ride $6; ✷ 11am-11pm Sun-Thu, 11am-midnight Fri & Sat; Ⓜ MGM Grand

Though your head and shoulders may take a beating, the heart-line twist-and-dive maneuver produces a sensation similar to that felt by a pilot during a barrel roll in a fighter plane. The rest of the four-minute ride includes stomach-dropping dipsy-dos, high-banked turns, a 540-degree spiral and blink-and-you'll-miss-it Strip views. Enter through the Coney Island Emporium arcade.

◉ RICHARD PETTY DRIVING EXPERIENCE

☎ 800-237-3889; www.1800bepetty .com; Las Vegas Motor Speedway, 6975 Speedway Blvd; ☽ varies, call for schedule

Curious about what it's like to be in high-speed pursuit? Here's your chance to ride shotgun during a Nascar-style qualifying run ($99) or drive yourself ($399) in a 600-horsepower stock car reaching speeds of over 150mph. Also at the Speedway, **Mario Andretti Racing School** (☎ 877-263-7388; http://andretti racing.com) offers cheaper ride-along and racing opportunities.

◉ STRATOSPHERE TOWER

Map p180

☎ 380-7777; www.stratospherehotel .com; Stratosphere, 2000 Las Vegas Blvd S; adult/concession elevator $10/6, incl 3 thrill rides $24/21; ☽ 10am-1am Sun-Thu, 10am-2am Fri & Sat

The world's highest thrill rides await, a whopping 110 stories above the Strip. Big Shot straps riders into completely exposed seats that zip up the tower's pinnacle, while Insanity spins riders out over the tower's edge. Views from X Scream are good, but the

ride itself is a dud – save your dough for Romance at Top of the World lounge (p129).

◉ VENETIAN GONDOLAS

Map p180

☎ 414-4500; www.venetian.com; Venetian, 3355 Las Vegas Blvd S; indoor/outdoor ride per person $12.50/15, private 2-passenger ride $50/60; ☽ departures 10am-10:45pm, to 11:45pm Fri & Sat, ticket booth opens at 9am/10am for indoor/outdoor rides; Ⓜ Harrah's/Imperial Palace

Graceful bridges, flowing canals, vibrant piazzas and stone walkways almost capture the romantic Venetian spirit inside the Grand Canal Shoppes (p80), especially when viewed from the seat of a floating gondola; same-day, in-person reservations required.

◉ SHOWY SPECTACULARS
◉ CIRCUS CIRCUS MIDWAY

Map p180

☎ 734-0410, 877-434-9175; www.circus circus.com; Circus Circus, 2880 Las Vegas Blvd S; admission free; ☽ shows every 30min 11am-midnight; 🚌 The Deuce

Free circus performances acts steal center stage directly above this Austin Powers–era casino's main floor. Grab a seat at the revolving Horse-A-Round Bar made infamous by Hunter S Thompson's gonzo-journalism epic *Fear and Loathing in Las Vegas*.

SEE | SHOP | EAT | PLAY

SEE

FOUNTAINS OF BELLAGIO
Map p182

☎ 693-7111; www.bellagio.com; Bellagio, 3600 Las Vegas Blvd S; admission free; ⏰ shows every 15min 8pm-midnight, every 30min 3-8pm Mon-Fri, noon-8pm Sat & Sun; Ⓜ Bally's & Paris

With a backdrop of Tuscan architecture, the Bellagio's artificial lake and dancing fountains are the antithesis of what most people expect from the desert. The fountain show's recorded soundtrack varies, so cross your fingers that it'll be Italian opera or ol' Blue Eyes crooning 'Luck Be a Lady.'

FREMONT STREET
EXPERIENCE Map pp184-5

☎ 678-5723; www.vegasexperience .com; admission free; ⏰ shows hourly 7pm-midnight; 🚌 The Deuce

The 1400ft (427m) canopy over downtown's Fremont St is steroid-enhanced by 550,000 watts of concert hall sound and a super-big Viva Vision screen. When the 12.5-million synchronized LEDs come on, cheesy sound-and-light shows are awesome enough to hypnotize every spectator (especially if you're tipsy).

MIRAGE VOLCANO Map p180

☎ 791-7111; www.mirage.com; Mirage, 3400 Las Vegas Blvd S; admission free; ⏰ shows hourly 8pm-midnight, starting 6pm/7pm in winter/spring; 🚌 The Deuce

TOP VEGAS FREEBIES

Strip Shows
> Circus Circus Midway (opposite)
> Fountains of Bellagio (left)
> Imperial Palace
  Dealertainers (p75)
> Mirage Volcano (left)
> Sirens of TI (p72)

Wild Wildlife
> Bellagio Conservatory & Botanical Gardens (p72)
> Flamingo Wildlife Habitat (p72)
> Lion Habitat at MGM Grand (p72)

Breakfast at Tiffany's
> Forum Shops at Caesars Palace (p80)
> Venetian's Grand Canal Shoppes (p80)
> Via Bellagio (p81)
> Wynn Esplanade (p82)

Doin' Downtown
> Fremont Street Experience (left)
> Main Street Station (p68)
> Neon Museum (p76)

Culture Vultures
> Arts Factory (p66)
> First Fridays (Commerce Street Studios, p67)
> Wynn Collection (p68)

For more ideas, see the 'For Free' suggested itinerary (p30).

When the Mirage's fiery trademark – a 100ft (30m) artificial volcano – erupts with a roar, it inevitably brings traffic on the Strip to a screeching halt. Be on the lookout for wisps of smoke escaping from the top that signal the fiery Polynesian inferno is about to begin.

⊙ SIRENS OF TI Map p180
☎ 894-7111; www.treasureisland.com; TI (Treasure Island), 3300 Las Vegas Blvd S; admission free; ⏱ 7pm, 8:30pm, 10pm & 11pm, weather permitting; 🚌 The Deuce

The laughably spicy Sirens of TI show, a mock sea battle fired up by pyrotechnics, witnesses a clash of the sexes pitting buxom temptresses against renegade freebooters in the cove outside TI (Treasure Island).

⊙ GARDENS & WILDLIFE

⊙ BELLAGIO CONSERVATORY & BOTANICAL GARDENS Map p182
☎ 693-7871 www.bellagio.com; Bellagio, 3600 Las Vegas Blvd S; admission free; ⏱ 24hr; Ⓜ Bally's & Paris

Adjacent to the hotel lobby, itself adorned with a backlit glass sculpture of 2000 vibrant hand-blown glass flowers, the Bellagio's conservatory houses bizarrely ostentatious floral arrangements that are installed by crane through the soaring 50ft (15m) ceiling.

⊙ FLAMINGO WILDLIFE HABITAT Map p182
☎ 733-3111; www.flamingolasvegas.com; 355 Las Vegas Blvd S; admission free; ⏱ 24hr; Ⓜ Flamingo/Caesars Palace

Step away from the gaming area into 15 acres of gardens, pools, waterfalls and waterways filled with swans, exotic birds and ornamental koi, where Chilean flamingos and African penguins wander around, and palm trees and jungle plants flourish in the midst of the Great Basin desert.

⊙ LION HABITAT AT MGM GRAND Map p182
☎ 891-7777; www.mgmgrand.com; MGM Grand, 3799 Las Vegas Blvd S; admission free; ⏱ 11am-10pm; 🚌 MGM Grand

MGM owns many of the magnificent felines, all descendants of the movie company's original mascot, but only two are shown off in this multimillion-dollar enclosure at any given time. The big cats sprawl atop a see-through walkway tunnel, separated from gawkers' heads by only a sheet of protective glass – and a couple of feet of air.

⊙ MIRAGE CASINO HOTEL Map p180
☎ 791-7111; www.mirage.com; Mirage, 3400 Las Vegas Blvd S; admission free; ⏱ 24hr; 🚌 The Deuce

This high-roller's casino is replete with a rainforest atrium under a 100ft (30m) conservatory dome filled with jungle foliage, meandering streams and soothing cascades. Woven into this waterscape are scores of bromeliads. Exotic scents waft through the hotel lobby, with its 20,000-gallon (75,708L) saltwater aquarium harboring five dozen species of tropical critters from pufferfish to pygmy sharks.

SHARK REEF Map p182
632-4555; www.mandalaybay.com; Mandalay Bay, 3950 Las Vegas Blvd S; adult/concession incl audioguide $16/11; 10am-11pm, last entry 10pm; The Deuce
Despite billboards advertising a great white shark looking oh-so-

menacing, you won't actually see any great whites at M-Bay. But this walk-through aquarium is home to over a thousand submarine beasties, including jellyfish, moray eels, stingrays and yes, some sharks. Other rare and endangered toothy reptiles on display include some of the world's last remaining golden crocodiles.

SIEGFRIED & ROY'S SECRET GARDEN & DOLPHIN HABITAT Map p180
791-7188; www.miragehabitat.com; Mirage, 3400 Las Vegas Blvd S; adult/concession $15/10; 11am-5:30pm Mon-Fri, 10am-5:30pm Sat & Sun, 10am-7pm daily in summer; The Deuce
All of the feats of conservation bragged about on the free

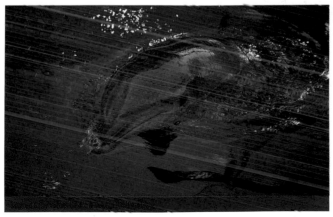

Greg Walker
'Dealertainer' at the Imperial Palace (opposite)

Thoughts on impersonating Elvis I'm not your typical Elvis impersonator, which is someone who really lives the life. I really love Elvis, but I don't have a shrine to him in my house. **Favorite Elvis song to sing** 'Viva Las Vegas,' because it is *so* Las Vegas and *so* Elvis. **How you got started in this biz** I started imitating famous people along with my brother and sister when we were kids, and we ended up having an act. **Other celebrities you've impersonated** Johnny Cash, Liberace, Rodney Dangerfield, Roy Orbison. **To be a great 'dealertainer' you need** Personality. Sociability. Know how to have fun playing a game, any game really. You laugh, you joke, you have your little rituals. **Strangest good-luck charm you've seen** Someone brought a wilted piece of lettuce to the blackjack table from the buffet! **Favorite casino game** Betting on football. **First-time visitors to Las Vegas shouldn't miss** The fountains of Bellagio (p71).

audio tour can't compensate for enclosures built much too small for animals who roam the world's wildest places, such as snow leopards, black jaguars, white lions and tigers. The Atlantic bottlenose dolphin pools are painfully cramped, too.

◎ QUIRKY LAS VEGAS

◎ IMPERIAL PALACE DEALERTAINERS Map p180
☎ 731-3311; www.imperialpalace .com; 3535 Las Vegas Blvd S; admission free; ⏰ shows every 30min noon-4am; Ⓜ Harrah's/Imperial Palace
Award-winning celebrity impersonators (p137) do double-duty as 'dealertainers,' jumping up from the blackjack tables to show off their song-and-dance skills on stage. Show up at 8pm for the shift change. Don't worry: Elvis never, ever leaves the building.

◎ LIBERACE MUSEUM Map pp190-1
☎ 798-5595; www.liberace.org; 1775 E Tropicana Ave; adult/concession $12.50/8.50; ⏰ 10am-5pm Tue-Sat, noon-4pm Sun; 🚌 free Strip shuttle, call for schedules
For connoisseurs of kitschy celebrity shrines, this place is a must-do. The home of 'Mr Showmanship' houses the most flamboyant art cars, outrageous costumes and ornate pianos you'll ever see. There's a hand-painted Pleyel, on which Chopin played; a Rolls-Royce covered

in mirrored tiles; and a wardrobe exhibit full of feathered capes and million-dollar furs, darling.

◎ MADAME TUSSAUDS LAS VEGAS Map p180
☎ 862-7800; www.madametussaudslv .com; 3377 Las Vegas Blvd S; adult $24, concession $14-18; ⏰ 10am-11pm; Ⓜ Harrah's/Imperial Palace
By the Venetian's moving Rialto Bridge walkway is this unique interactive wax museum, where you can strike a pose with Elvis, play golf with Tiger Woods or put on Playboy bunny ears and sit on Hugh Hefner's lap (make sure you touch him, since Hef's made of silicone – how appropo!)

◎ MUSEUM OF THE AMERICAN COCKTAIL Map p180
☎ 892-8272; www.museumoftheam ericancocktail.org; inside Commander's Palace, Desert Passage, 3663 Las Vegas Blvd S; admission free; ⏰ 9am-9pm; 🚌 The Deuce
Delve into the liquid origins of American mixology, from the pre-Prohibition era to the modern day. Witty historical exhibits fill an elegant side lounge at Commander's Palace restaurant, which offers 25¢ martini weekday lunches to put your newly acquired knowledge to immediate use. Check online for cocktail seminar schedules and to see if the museum has found a new permanent home.

◉ NEON MUSEUM Map pp184-5

☎ 387-6366; www.neonmuseum.org; Neonopolis, 450 E Fremont St S; admission free; ☽ 24hr; 🚌 The Deuce

Plaques tell the story of each sign at this alfresco assemblage of vintage neon. Genie lamps, glowing martini glasses and 1940s motel marquees brighten up this otherwise bleak slice of downtown, especially inside the Neonopolis and on alleys of Fremont St further west. Tours of the giant 'boneyard' of rescued signs are by appointment only.

◉ PINBALL HALL OF FAME
Map pp178-9

www.pinballmuseum.org; 3330 E Tropicana Ave, at Pecos Rd; admission free, games 25-50¢; ☽ 11am-11pm Sun-Thu, 11am-midnight Fri & Sat; 🚌 201

Next to a discount cinema far east of the Strip, this wacky museum lets you play its vintage pinball, video-arcade and carnival fortune-teller games, all dating from the 1950s to the '90s. Don't forget to read the handwritten cards curating the priceless collection. Profits from every quarter you drop into the slots go to charity.

◉ SLOTS-A-FUN Map p180

☎ 734-0410; 2890 Las Vegas Blvd S; admission free; ☽ 24hr; 🚌 The Deuce; 🅿 at Circus Circus

For cheap booze and cheap thrills, it's tough to beat this lowbrow

dive. Grab a coupon book, give the giant slot machine two free spins, and scarf down a few 75¢ beers and $1 half-pound hot dogs. Then kick back, relax and enjoy the laughable lounge acts.

◉ STAR TREK: THE EXPERIENCE Map pp190-1

☎ 888-462-6535; www.startrekexp .com; Hilton, 3000 Paradise Rd; museum & unlimited motion-simulator rides adult/concession $39/36, tours $32-40; ☽ daily; Ⓜ Las Vegas Hilton

Cruise on impulse power through the museum-of-the-future exhibit, featuring authentic *Star Trek* props. Then queue for the live-action motion-simulation rides: the newer 'Borg Invasion 4-D' and the classic 'Klingon Encounter' aboard – what else? – the starship *Enterprise*. 'Secrets Unveiled' tours go behind the scenes of this $70-million interactive attraction, which includes Quark's Bar (p123) and Deep Space Nine Promenade (p88).

◉ WEDDING CHAPELS

Before you get hitched (p24), stop by Clark County's **Marriage Bureau** (☎ 671-0600; www.co.clark.nv.us/clerk /marriage_information.htm; 201 Clark Ave; ☽ 8am-midnight) for a license ($55, cash only). Civil courthouse ceremonies are performed 8am to 10pm daily. Many casino hotels also have themed wedding chapels.

A SPECIAL MEMORY WEDDING CHAPEL Map pp186-7
☎ 800-962-7798; www.aspecialmemory.com; 800 S 4th St; 🕑 8am-10pm Sun-Thu, 8am-midnight Fri & Sat; 🚌 The Deuce

The drive-up window on Lovers Lane has a wedding menu board (breakfast packages cost from $55, plus don't forget to tip the minister). A limo ride or an appearance by Elvis, Marilyn Monroe or Grandpa Munster are à la carte.

GRACELAND WEDDING CHAPEL Map pp186-7
☎ 382-0091, 800-824-5732; www.gracelandchapel.com; 619 Las Vegas Blvd S; 🕑 8am-midnight; 🚌 The Deuce

Offering the original Elvis impersonator wedding (from $199) for over 50 years. If it's good enough for Jon Bon Jovi, then it's probably good enough for you, too.

LITTLE CHURCH OF THE WEST Map p182
☎ 739-7971, 800-821-2452; www.littlechurchlv.com; 4617 Las Vegas Blvd S; 🕑 8am-midnight; 🚌 The Deuce

If we ever get married in Vegas, this is where you'll find us: in a quiet little wooden chapel built in 1942, in the shadow of the South Strip, as seen in the classic Elvis movie *Viva Las Vegas*. Beginners' wedding packages from $199.

MAVERICK HELICOPTERS
☎ 261-0007, 888-261-4414; www.maverickhelicopter.com; 6705 Las Vegas Blvd S; 🕑 by reservation only; 🚌 The Deuce

Take flight with Grand Canyon (p145) or Valley of Fire (p144) wedding package, or stage a sunset ceremony cruise on Lake Mead in your own private yacht. Packages cost from $699.

VIVA LAS VEGAS WEDDINGS Map pp186-7
☎ 384-0771, 800-574-4450; www.vivalasvegasweddings.com; 1205 Las Vegas Blvd S; 🕑 9am-5pm; 🚌 The Deuce

Even if you're not contemplating tying the knot, it's worth a peek inside to see if anyone is getting married – the public is welcome at the wackily themed wedding ceremonies (imagine vampires, Harley hogs or Cirque du Soleil-esque aerial acrobats), which are broadcast live online. More traditional wedding packages cost from $199.

WEE KIRK O' THE HEATHER Map pp184-5
☎ 382-9830, 800-843-5266; www.weekirk.com; 231 Las Vegas Blvd S; 🕑 10am-8pm; 🚌 The Deuce

The oldest continuously operating wedding chapel in Las Vegas (since 1940), and it's conveniently close to the county marriage bureau. Quaint, romantic wedding packages cost from just $49.

🏠 SHOP

In the city of 'Lost Wages,' consumption is as wildly conspicuous as dancing fountains in the middle of the desert. Upscale international haute purveyors cater to the cashed-up – you can find almost anything that you'd find in London, New York or Tokyo, plus a few unique high-roller items not likely to be sold anytime soon.

If all you really want is a T-shirt, coffee mug or bumper sticker announcing to the world that you've finally been to 'Fabulous Las Vegas,' they're everywhere you turn. But if you're looking for something more unusual, specialty shops are stuffed full of cool kitsch and priceless collectibles, from vintage casino memorabilia to wacky shot glasses and showgirls' feather boas.

The Vegas Valley has over 30 million sq ft (2.8 million sq m) of retail space. Most merchants can arrange to have your goodies shipped home. Retail shopping hours are normally 10am to 9pm (to 6pm Sunday), but casino shops, arcades and malls typically stay open until 11pm or midnight. Christmas is one of the few holidays for which most shops close.

SHOPPING AREAS

Megaresort casino hotels dominate the scene. The Strip is the focus of the shopping action, with upscale boutiques blooming in the newer resorts from Wynn south to Mandalay Place. Downtown and the Westside are the places to cruise for wigs, naughty adult goods and trashy lingerie. Vintage clothing stores, antiques shops and art galleries are reviving the Naked City, especially around the intersection of Charleston and Las Vegas Blvds. On the Eastside near UNLV, Maryland Parkway is chock-a-block with hip shops catering to the college crowd. Trendy one-off boutiques are scarce, but they're popping up in outlying suburbs, where discount outlet malls are found.

Top left Exotic cars at the Forum Shops (p80), Caesars Palace **Top right** Forum Shops **Bottom** Fashion Show (p80)

SEE | SHOP | EAT | PLAY

SHOP

SHOPPING MALLS & ARCADES

THE DISTRICT Map pp178-9
☎ 564-8595, 877-564-8595; www.the
districtatgvr.com; Green Valley Ranch,
2240 Village Walk Dr, Henderson, off I-215
exit Green Valley Parkway; ⏰ 10am-9pm
Mon-Sat, 11am-7pm Sun; 🚌 111
An off-Strip shopping magnet, the
open-air District has a cool mix of
five dozen shops, including indie
designer boutiques and REI, the
West Coast outdoor sports retailer.
A free trolley makes the rounds
every 15 minutes.

FASHION SHOW Map p180
☎ 369-0704; www.thefashionshow
.com; 3200 Las Vegas Blvd S; ⏰ 10am-
9pm Mon-Fri, 10am-8pm Sat, 11am-7pm
Sun; 🚌 The Deuce
Size *does* matter. Though unique
shops are sparse at Nevada's biggest and flashiest mall, there are
250 chain storefronts, all anchored
by giant department stores. Movie
stars drop by Talulah G and Still
boutiques, while models hit the
runway Friday, Saturday and Sunday afternoons. It's topped off by
'The Cloud,' a multimedia canopy
resembling a flamenco hat.

FORUM SHOPS Map p182
☎ 893-4800; www.simon.com; Caesars
Palace, 3500 Las Vegas Blvd S; ⏰ 10am-
11pm Sun-Thu, to midnight Fri & Sat;
Ⓜ Flamingo/Caesars Palace

Hundred-dollar bills fly out of
Fendi bags faster here than in
the high-roller casinos. Caesars'
fanciful re-creation of an ancient
Roman marketplace houses 160
designer emporia, including one-
name catwalk wonders such as
Armani, Versace and DKNY, and
specialty boutiques such as Exotic
Cars (p85) and Playboy. Don't
miss the spiral escalator, a grand
entrance for divas just sauntering
in off the Strip.

GRAND CANAL SHOPPES
Map p180
☎ 414-4500; www.venetian.com; Venetian, 3355 Las Vegas Blvd S; ⏰ 10am-
11pm Sun-Thu, to midnight Fri & Sat;
Ⓜ Harrah's/Imperial Palace
Wandering minstrels, jugglers
and laughable living statues
inhabit this Italianate indoor mall.
Cobblestone walkways wind past
BCBG Max Azaria, Godiva, Kenneth
Cole, Jimmy Choo, Sephora and 90
other luxury shops. The doors are
thrown open for early-bird window shopping at 7am. Don't want
to walk? Take a leisurely gondola
ride (p70).

HARD ROCK Map pp190-1
☎ 693-5000; Hard Rock, 4455 Paradise
Rd; ⏰ most shops 10am-11pm Sun-Thu,
to 1am Fri & Sat; 🚌 108, 202
For hard-to-find rock-star clothing
brands and rare collectibles, swing

by this off-Strip casino's logo shop. Then pop into Lov Jones for imported lingerie; the cigar humidor at Cuba Libre, which has a bar serving vintage scotch and cognac; and Rocks, a 24-hour jewelry store, to pick up that diamond watch right after your big win at poker.

⌂ MANDALAY PLACE Map p182
☎ 632-9333; skybridge btwn Mandalay Bay & Luxor, 3930 Las Vegas Blvd S; ☼ 10am-11pm; ▢ The Deuce

M-Bay's airy commercial promenade houses 40 unique, fashion-forward boutiques, including Samantha Chang, GF Ferré, Oilily, Sauvage, Urban Outfitters, Lunettes, Chocolate Swan, The Art of Shaving and the first-ever Nike Golf store. Revel in the de-stress atmosphere and vaulted ceilings.

⌂ MIRACLE MILE SHOPS
Map p182
☎ 888-800-8284; www.canyouhandle thismuchshopping.com; Planet Hollywood 3663 Las Vegas Blvd S; ☼ 10am-10pm Sun-??? to midnight Fri & Sat; Ⓜ Bally's & Paris

Formerly the Aladdin's North African -themed marketplace, this sleekly redesigned mall is a staggering 1.5 miles (2.4km) long. With over 170 retailers and 15 restaurants, the focus remains on contemporary chains, notably urban apparel, jewelry and gifts. Cargo bikes can be hired to transport baggage-laden shoppers to the remote parking garage.

⌂ VIA BELLAGIO Map p182
☎ 693-7111; www.bellagio.com; Bellagio, 3600 Las Vegas Blvd S; ☼ 10am-midnight; Ⓜ Bally's & Paris

BLUE LIGHT SPECIALS

Brand-name bargain hunters can save a lotta moolah at these jam-packed outlet malls:

Fashion Outlet Mall (☎ 874-1400, 888-424-6898; www.fashionoutletlasvegas.com; 32100 Las Vegas Blvd S, off I 15 exit 1, Primm; ☼ 10am-8pm) A 30-minute drive southwest of Las Vegas, at the Nevada/California state line, there's an excellent mix of over 80 high-end (Coach, Versace, Neiman Marcus Last Call, Tommy Hilfiger) and everyday (Banana Republic, Gap, Sketchers) brands. It's accessible from the Strip via a shoppers shuttle (round trip $15) that departs five times daily from the MGM Grand.

Las Vegas Premium Outlets (Map pp186-7; ☎ 474-7500; www.premiumoutlets.com; 875 S Grand Central Parkway; ☼ 10am-9pm Mon-Sat, 10am-8pm Sun) The most upscale of Vegas' outlet malls features 120 high-end names such as Armani Exchange, Calvin Klein, Coach, Dolce & Gabbana and Guess, along with a few midrange options like Levi's and Adidas. CAT's Downtown Shoppers Express shuttle serves the mall every 20 minutes from 10am until 5pm.

Bellagio's swish indoor promenade is home to the who's who of fashion-plate designers: Armani, Chanel, Dior, Fred Leighton (opposite), Gucci, Hermès, Prada, Tiffany & Co and Yves Saint Laurent. Bring a pocket pooch and your darkest celebrity-in-disguise sunglasses.

🛍 WYNN ESPLANADE Map p180
☎ 770-7000; www.wynnlasvegas.com; Wynn, 3131 Las Vegas Blvd S; ☽ 10am-11pm Sun-Thu, to midnight Fri & Sat; 🚇 The Deuce

Steve Wynn's new eponymous blockbuster resort showcases 75,000 sq ft (nearly 7000 sq m) of consumer bliss, with top-of-the-line retailers such as Chanel, Cartier, Dior, Jean-Paul Gaultier and Manolo Blahnik, plus the high-tech toy store Gizmos. After you hit the jackpot, take a test drive at the Ferarri-Maserati dealership.

🛍 CLOTHING & JEWELRY

Look for star-powered LA boutique Fred Segal at the new W Las Vegas casino hotel, slated to open in 2009.

🛍 ATTIC Map pp186-7
☎ 388-4088; www.theatticlasvegas .com; 1018 S Main St; ☽ 10am-5pm Mon-Thu, 10am-6pm Fri, 11am-6pm Sat; 🚌 108, 207

A $1 'lifetime pass' (applied to your first purchase) is required to enter this vintage emporium, but it's worth it, even if you don't buy anything. Be mesmerized by fabulous hats, outrageous wigs, hippie-chic clubwear and retro furnishings. An upstairs coffee bar serves invigorating salads and sandwiches.

🛍 BUFFALO EXCHANGE
Map pp190-1
☎ 791-3960; www.buffaloexchange .com; 4110 S Maryland Parkway; ☽ 10am-8pm Mon-Sat, 11am-7pm Sun; 🚌 109, 202

Trade in your nearly new garb for cash or credit at this savvy second-hand chain. Don't worry: they've combed through the dingy thrift-store stuff and culled only the best 1940s to '70s vintage, clubwear, costuming goodies and designer duds.

🛍 D'LOE HOUSE OF STYLE
Map pp186-7
☎ 382-5688; www.houseofstylethen andnow.com; 220 E Charleston Blvd; ☽ noon-6:30pm Mon-Sat; 🚌 105, 206

You'll know it's fabulous as soon as you catch sight of the hot-pink-and-blue exterior. It's owned by Cirque du Soleil costume designer Mario D'Loe, who hoards unique fashions from the pre-WWII era to the 1970s, including evening wear and bejeweled accessories. Brad Pitt and the Killers have been spotted modeling vintage shirts found here.

SHOP > MUSIC & BOOKS

☐ FRED LEIGHTON Map p180
☎ 693-7050; Via Bellagio, 3600 Las Vegas Blvd S; 🕙 10am-midnight; Ⓜ Bally's & Paris

Many Academy Awards–night adornments are on loan from the world's most prestigious collection of antique jewelry, notably art deco and art nouveau. In Las Vegas, unlike at the uptight NYC outlet, they'll let anyone try on finery that once belonged to royalty. Pricetags easily top $1 million at this veritable museum of jewels.

☐ VALENTINO'S ZOOTSUIT CONNECTION Map pp180-7
☎ 383-9555; 906 S 6th St; 🕙 11am-5pm Mon-Sat; 🚌 The Deuce

Lots of timeless glam duds get cast off in this ahistorical town. Some end up at this upscale resale boutique, which specializes in men's and women's clothing from the 1930s, '40s and '50s. Rentals, custom zootsuits, cocktail dresses, collectible tiepins and felt hats are specialties.

☐ WILLIAMS COSTUME COMPANY Map pp186-7
☎ 384-1384; 1226 S 3rd St; 🕙 10am-5:15pm Mon-Sat; 🚌 105

Williams has supplied the Strip's starlets with DIY costuming goods for over half a century. Check out the headshots in the dressing rooms, then pick up some rhine-

---

MORE BLING BLING THAN DING DING DING

Witness **Prada** (☎ 866-6886) at Via Bellagio; **Jimmy Choo** at the Forum Shops (☎ 691-2097) and Grand Canal Shoppes (☎ 733-1802); **Versace** (☎ 792-9372) at the Forum Shops; **Manolo Blahnik** (☎ 770-0000) at Wynn Esplanade; **Dolce & Gabbana** (☎ 732-9292) at the Forum Shops; and **Tiffany & Co** (☎ 697-5400) at Via Bellagio. Most megaresorts have jewelry stores with lovely adornments, such as **Cartier** (☎ 733-6652) at Caesars Palace. Technosexuals gravitate toward the **Apple Store** (☎ 650-9550) at the Fashion Show and **Sony Style** (☎ 697-5420) at the Forum Shops.

---

stories, sequins, feathers etc – you go, girlfriend. Costume rentals are available, too.

MUSIC & BOOKS
For riveting reads about Las Vegas, see p157.

☐ ALTERNATE REALITY COMICS Map pp190-1
☎ 736-3673; www.alternaterealitycomics.net; 4800 S Maryland Parkway; 🕙 11am-7pm Wed-Sat, noon-6pm Sun-Tue; 🚌 109

In the same UNLV strip mall as a tattoo parlor and indie vinyl shop, this unbelievably cool comic shop fills its shelves with graphic novels,

SEE | SHOP | EAT | PLAY

SHOP

Japanese manga and collectibles for geek connoisseurs.

GAMBLER'S BOOK SHOP
Map pp186-7

☎ 382-7555, 800-522-1777; www.gamblersbook.com; 630 S 11th St; 🕙 9am-5pm Mon-Sat; 🚌 109, 206

Owner Edna Luckman (no joke) stocks thousands of gaming strategy books, including out-of-print titles. The staff, some of whom look as if they might have been around since the Rat Pack era, can dispense valuable advice.

READING ROOM Map p182

☎ 632-9374; Mandalay Place, 3930 S Las Vegas Blvd; 🕙 10am-11pm; 🚌 The Deuce

The Strip's only independent bookseller is also the city's best. Bookworms will be hypnotized by the thoughtful selection of hot-off-the-press books about Vegas, plus some rare and collectible editions. Author readings and book signings take place here.

ZIA RECORDS Map pp190-1

☎ 735-4942; www.ziarecords.com; 4225 S Eastern Ave; 🕙 10am-midnight; 🚌 110, 202

Calling itself the 'last real record store,' this Arizona-based vendor has a warehouse full of ear-tickling sounds, including a locals-only section where you just might dig up a demo by the next breakout Vegas band. Live in-store performances

Reading Room, Mandalay Place

happen on a stage with the warning sign: 'No moshing allowed.'

SPECIALIST STORES

55° WINE + DESIGN Map p182
☎ 632-9355; Mandalay Place, 3930 Las Vegas Blvd S; ⏰ 10am-11pm; 🚌 The Deuce

Exclusive wine bottles are stacked inside mod white fiberglass pods, alongside priceless handmade glassware and accessories at this classy wine store. Knowledgeable staff pour at the tasting bar and escort oenophiles through a refrigerated wine cellar that stocks 2000 truly international vintages. Every bottle that you buy even gets its own air-cushioned takeout bag!

ANTIQUES DISTRICT
Map pp186-7

An offbeat antiques district has taken shape just south of downtown in a series of funky stores inside older homes. Places worth checking out include the supermod **Funk House** (☎ 678-6278; www .thefunkhouselasvegas.com; 1228 S Casino Center Blvd; ⏰ 10am-5pm) and shabby-chic **Gypsy Caravan** (☎ 868-3302; 1302 S 3rd St; ⏰ 10am-5pm Tue-Sat).

AUTO COLLECTIONS Map p180
☎ 794-3174; www.autocollections .com; Imperial Palace, 5th fl, 3535 Las Vegas Blvd S; adult/concession $7/3, free coupons on website; ⏰ 9:30am-9:30pm; Ⓜ Harrah's & Imperial Palace

Car buffs could easily pass away an afternoon drooling over one of the world's largest privately owned auto collections. Among the prized vehicles that are on hand here (all for sale) are more Rolls-Royces than you can toss a chauffeur at.

CASA FUENTE Map p182
☎ 731-5051; Caesars Palace, 3500 Las Vegas Blvd S; ⏰ 10am-11pm Sun-Thu, to midnight Fri & Sat; Ⓜ Flamingo/Caesars Palace

A million-dollar cigar shop with a bar that feels like a little slice of Havana; the walk-in humidor contains signature stogies from the Dominican Republic and around the world (except Cuba, of course – damn those US customs regulations!). Order a tropical cocktail from the petite bar.

EXOTIC CARS Map p182
☎ 893-4800; Forum Shops, Caesars Palace, 3500 Las Vegas Blvd S; admission $5; ⏰ 10am-11pm Sun-Thu, to midnight Fri & Sat; Ⓜ Flamingo/Caesars Palace

Almost more of an attraction than a bi-level retail shop; here you can peruse Porsche-brand apparel, get your photo taken inside a Ferrari and salivate over a racier lifestyle. Around 50 vehicles are on display, some easily worth up to a million dollars.

HOUDINI'S MAGIC SHOP
Map p182

☎ 893-4800; www.houdini.com; Forum Shops, Caesars Palace, 3500 Las Vegas Blvd S; ⏲ 10am-11pm Sun-Thu, to midnight Fri & Sat; Ⓜ Flamingo/Caesars Palace
The legendary escape artist's legacy lives on at this shop packed with gags, pranks and magic tricks. Tuxedoed magicians perform for free and every purchase includes a free private lesson in the secretive back room. Also at New York-New York (p49) and the Venetian (p43).

METROPOLITAN MUSEUM OF ART STORE Map p182
☎ 691-2506; Miracle Mile, Planet Hollywood, 3663 Las Vegas Blvd S; ⏲ 10am-10pm Sun-Thu, to midnight Fri & Sat; ☐ The Deuce

NYC's Met is known for its reproductions and singular gift items. Sales of books, prints and jewelry support the museum's high-culture mission.

NIKETOWN Map p182
☎ 650-8888; Forum Shops, Caesars Palace, 3500 Las Vegas Blvd S; ⏲ 10am-11pm Sun-Thu, to midnight Fri & Sat; Ⓜ Flamingo/Caesars Palace
The sporty kicks might not help you jump higher, but they will certainly send your credit-card bill soaring. A sociable running club convenes here every Wednesday at 6pm. For couch-potato sports fans, the memorabilia and video screens are worth a look.

RED ROOSTER ANTIQUE MALL Map pp186-7
☎ 382-5253; 1109 Western Ave; ⏲ 10am-6pm Mon-Sat, 11am-5pm Sun; ☐ 108, 206
Located in the lowly shadow of the interstate, here at this one-stop retro extravaganza the

TOP FIVE ONLY-IN-VEGAS SHOPS
> Exotic Cars (p85)
> Gambler's Book Shop (p84)
> Gamblers General Store (p88)
> Rainbow Feather Co (p88)
> Showcase Slots (p89)

vintage tiki-wares draw shoppers from as far away as Hawaii. Keep a sharp eye out for Rat Pack–era memorabilia. It's a bit tricky to get here, so telephone first for directions.

🛍 NAUGHTY NOVELTIES

There are full-service lingerie shops inside many strip clubs (p134). All those hard-working beefy guys and sultry women obviously don't have time to make their own G-strings and tasseled undies!

🛍 ADULT SUPERSTORE
Map pp188-9
☎ 798-0144; 3850 W Tropicana Ave; ⏰ 24hr; 🚌 201
This enormous, well-lit porn warehouse has more pussies than the SPCA: toys, books, magazines, videos, tasteful 'marital enhancement products' and titillating accessories. Solo guys gravitate toward the XXX arcade upstairs.

🛍 BARE ESSENTIALS/
FANTASY FASHIONS Map pp188-9
☎ 247-4711; www.bareessentialsvegas .com; 4029 W Sahara Ave; ⏰ 10am-7pm Mon-Sat, noon-5pm Sun; 🚌 204
Pros swear by BE for business attire. It's heavy on theme wear – lots of cheerleader and schoolgirl outfits. Next-door **Bad Attitude Boutique** (☎ 646-9669; www.badattitude

.com; ⏰ noon-6pm Mon-Sat) makes custom-made corsets, goth fetish wear and burlesque fashions, while neighboring **Red Shoes** (☎ 889-4442; ⏰ 11am-8pm Mon-Sat, noon-7:30pm Sun) stocks knee-high boots and glittery platforms.

🛍 PARADISE ELECTRO
STIMULATIONS Map pp186-7
☎ 474-2991, 800-339-6953; www .pcselectro.com; 1509 W Oakey Blvd; ⏰ 10am-7pm Mon-Fri, noon-5pm Sat; 🚌 105
The 'Tiffany's of Fetish Boutiques' is tucked discreetly away on the wrong side of the tracks. It's the exotic, erotic and invigorating home of owner Dante Amore's legendary Auto-Erotic Chair, which must be seen (and felt) to be believed. Yeeowch.

🛍 SLIGHTLY SINFUL Map pp186-7
☎ 387-1006; 1232 Las Vegas Blvd S; ⏰ noon-10pm Sun-Thu, to midnight Fri & Sat; 🚌 The Deuce
For voyeurs, admiring the trashy stripper worthly apparel in the presence of the, ahem, professional clientele can make a visit worth the effort.

🛍 STRINGS OF LAS VEGAS
Map pp188-9
☎ 873-7820; www.exoticdanceware store.com; 4970 Arville St; ⏰ 10am-9pm Mon-Sat, 1-7pm Sun; 🚌 104, 201

SEE | SHOP | EAT | PLAY

SHOP

It's no surprise to see a Hummer limo pulling up outside this industrial warehouse of adult and fetish fashions. Watch go-go dancers get dressed (or undressed, rather) from head to toe here, with jewelry, platform shoes and the shortest skirts and scantiest G-strings you've ever seen. Custom-made costume designs sold.

WEIRD & WONDERFUL

You can find quirky Atomic Age reproduction collectibles, books and movies at the Atomic Testing Museum (p66).

BONANZA GIFTS Map p180
☎ 385-7359; www.worldslargest giftshop.com; 2440 Las Vegas Blvd S; 🕘 8am-midnight; Ⓜ Sahara
It's not the 'World's Largest Gift Shop' as it claims to be, but the amazing selection of only-in-Vegas souvenirs includes entire aisles of dice clocks, snow globes, slogan T-shirts, shot glasses and XXX gags.

DEEP SPACE NINE PROMENADE Map pp190-1
☎ 888-462-6535; www.startrekexp .com; Las Vegas Hilton, 3000 Paradise Rd; 🕘 11am-10pm Sun-Thu, to 11pm Fri & Sat; Ⓜ Las Vegas Hilton
Trekkies will think they've died and gone to Sto-vo-kor. Authentic TV and movie props, stuffed tribbles, Klingon ale and autographed

collectibles found nowhere else in the Alpha or even Delta quadrants cost from just a few Earth dollars up to several hundred bars of gold-pressed latinum.

GAMBLERS GENERAL STORE Map pp186-7
☎ 382-9903, 800-322-2447; www .gamblersgeneralstore.com; 800 S Main St; 🕘 9am-6pm; 🚍 108, 207
This authentic gambling supply store has it all, from custom-made chips to roulette wheels and poker tables identical to those found in many casinos. It's also perfect for cheapo souvenirs like decks of cards once used in actual casinos on the Strip.

GUN STORE Map pp190-1
☎ 454-1110; www.thegunstorelas vegas.com; 2900 E Tropicana Ave; 🕘 9am-6:30pm; 🚍 201
Attention wannabe Schwarzeneggers: this high-powered shop offers live submachine-gun and pistol rentals to fire off in its indoor training range, not to mention a massive cache of weapons for sale.

RAINBOW FEATHER CO
Map pp186-7
☎ 598-0988; www.rainbowfeatherco .com; 1036 S Main St; 🕘 9am-4pm Mon-Fri, 9am-1pm Sat; 🚍 108
Where to satisfy that boa fetish? Need turkey, chicken, duck, goose,

pheasant, ostrich or peacock quills? Rainbow stocks a positively fabulous selection of fine feathers in every possible shade.

⬚ SERGE'S SHOWGIRL WIGS
Map pp190-1
☎ 732-1015, 800-947-9447; www.show girlwigs.com; Commercial Center, 953 E Sahara Ave; ☼ 10am-5:30pm Mon-Sat; 🚌 204

In a trashy strip mall east of the Sahara casino hotel, Serge's friendly staff of stylists readily help Vegas showgirls, drag queens and even little ol' you find a whole new glamour girl inside themselves.

⬚ SHOWCASE SLOTS Map pp188-9
☎ 888-522-7568; www.showcaseslots .com; 2600 W Sahara Ave; ☼ 9am-5pm Mon-Sat; 🚌 204

Sock away spare change in your own stylish piggy bank: buy a vintage or modern one-armed bandit or video-poker machine. They sell nostalgic game-room antiques like Wurlitzer jukeboxes and retro candy machines, too. Also in the Miracle Mile Shops (p81).

🍴 EAT

Although the heydays of Vegas dinner shows may be over, showmanship is still a high priority. After Wolfgang Puck brought Spago to Caesars Palace in 1992, celebrity American chefs opened branches at every megaresort. Casino restaurants all competed to dream up the next big attraction. Recently Las Vegas has witnessed an invasion of French chefs, who have taken desert dining to a stratospheric level.

With so many tables to choose from, the stakes are high and there are many overhyped eating gambles. Cheap buffets and meal deals still exist, mostly downtown and at less glitzy Strip addresses. It's slim pickings for vegetarians, but there are typically a few menu options at most places.

Every major casino hotel has a 24 hour café; breakfast is often served nonstop. Weekend champagne brunch buffets (9am to 4pm) are a hot ticket. Lunch is 11am to 3pm. Dinner is 5pm to 10pm weekdays, to 11pm weekends.

Book as far in advance as you can for pricier restaurants. Reservations at the biggest names are crucial, especially weekends. At the most famous places, jackets are required for men.

The standard gratuity is 15% to 20% before tax. A service charge of 15% to 18% is often added for groups of six or more; don't double tip. At buffets, leave at least $1 per person on the table.

MEAL COSTS

The pricing symbols used in this book indicate the cost of a main dinner course, excluding tax, tips or drinks.

$	under $10
$$	$10-24
$$$	$25-40
$$$$	over $40

Top left Village Eateries (p101), New York-New York

SEE | SHOP | EAT | PLAY

EAT

THE STRIP

 BALLY'S

▐ STERLING BRUNCH Map p182
Buffet $$$$

☎ 967-7999; Bally's Steakhouse, 3645 Las Vegas Blvd S; ⏱ 9:30am-2:30pm Sun; Ⓜ Bally's & Paris

Indulge in the best – and most expensive – Sunday champagne brunch in town. Ice sculptures and lavish flower arrangements abound, as do food stations featuring broiled lobster, caviar on ice – you get the idea. Reservations recommended.

 BELLAGIO

The Bellagio's roster of culinary heavyweights features over a half-dozen James Beard Award winners. For reservations visit the website www.bellagio.com, or call ☎ 877-234-6358. Note that children are not permitted at many restaurants.

▐ BUFFET Map p182
Buffet $$-$$$

☎ 693-7111; Bellagio, 3600 Las Vegas Blvd S; ⏱ 8am-10:30am & 11am-3pm Mon-Fri, 8am-3:30pm Sat & Sun, 4-10pm Mon-Thu, 4:30-11pm Fri & Sat, 4:30-10:30pm Sun; Ⓜ Bally's & Paris; ♿ Ⓥ

The Bellagio competes for top honors for Vegas' best live-action buffet. The sumptuous all-you-can-eat spread includes such crowd-pleasers as smoked salmon, duck and innumerable creative dishes from all around the globe. Go for lunch, the best value.

▐ CIRCO Map p182
Northern Italian $$$

☎ 693-8150; Bellagio, 3600 Las Vegas Blvd S; ⏱ 5:30-10:30pm; Ⓜ Bally's & Paris

This whimsical Big Top–inspired *osteria* overlooks the dancing fountains of faux Lake Como. Rustic yet complex handmade pasta and *secondi* such as Tuscan octopus and calamari stew perform well alongside an international wine cellar. Reservations suggested.

▐ FIX Map p182
New American $$$

☎ 693-8400; www.lightgroup.com; Bellagio, 3600 Las Vegas Blvd S; ⏱ 5pm-midnight Sun-Thu, to 2am Fri & Sat; Ⓜ Bally's & Paris

A perfect pre-clubbing launch pad, or just for eyeing celebs and the casino floor, this trendy, high-flying kitchen makes gourmet comfort-food goodies like roasted tomato soup with a grilled aged cheddar-cheese sandwich, Kobe beef sliders with spicy fries and choco-java 'shake & cake.' Reservations recommended.

LE CIRQUE Map p182
Contemporary French $$$$
☎ 693-7223; Bellagio, 3600 Las Vegas Blvd S; 🕑 5:30-10pm; Ⓜ Bally's & Paris
An outpost of the legendary NYC restaurant pairs artful haute cuisine with world-class wines in a joyous, intimate lakeside setting with a silk-tented ceiling. Foie gras terrine, roasted truffle-skin chicken and roasted duck with Tasmanian honey are among the signature dishes. Three-ring tasting menu $98, five acts $125. Jacket and tie preferred. Reservations essential.

OLIVES Map p182
Mediterranean $$$
☎ 693-8181; www.toddenglish.com; Via Bellagio, Bellagio, 3600 Las Vegas Blvd S; 🕑 11am-2:30pm & 5-10:30pm Mon-Thu, 11am-10:30pm Fri-Sun; Ⓜ Bally's & Paris; Ⓥ
East Coast chef Todd English dishes up a homage to the ancient life-giving fruit. Flatbread pizzas, housemade pastas and flame-licked meats get top billing. The chef's table faces a bustling open kitchen; patio tables overlook Lake Como. Good wine list, flamboyant desserts. Reservations necessary.

PICASSO Map p182
French/Mediterranean $$$$
☎ 693-8105; Via Bellagio, Bellagio, 3600 Las Vegas Blvd S; 🕑 6-9:30pm Wed-Mon; Ⓜ Bally's & Paris
Five-star chef Julian Serrano delivers artistic Franco-Iberian fusion in a museum-like setting with vaulted ceilings. Original eponymous masterpieces don't overshadow entrées like sautéed fallow deer medallions or seafood *boudin*. Linger on the lakeside patio over a *digestif*. Prix fixe menus ($95 to $105) recommended. Jacket and tie suggested. Reservations essential but difficult.

BEST RABELAISIAN FEASTS
When it comes to groaning boards, the old adage 'You get what you pay for' was never more true. More expensive buffets feature live-action stations specializing in omelets, pastas, stir-fries and so on. At opulent megaresorts, you should salivate over shrimp, lobster claws, antipasti, carved-to-order roast meats, fresh fruit, various soups and lots of salads. The Wynn (p106), Bellagio (opposite), Paris (p102) and Rio (p114) buffets compete for top honors, with the Mirage (p100) and TI (Treasure Island, p103) running close behind. On Sundays, Bally's (p92) lays out the best champagne spread, while the House of Blues (p126) gospel brunch and Commander's Palace (p102) Dixieland jazz brunch are stand-outs.

SEE | SHOP | EAT | PLAY

EAT

🍴 PRIME STEAKHOUSE Map p182
Steakhouse/Seafood $$$-$$$$
☎ 877-234-6358; Via Bellagio, Bellagio, 3600 Las Vegas Blvd S; ⏰ 5-10pm; Ⓜ Bally's & Paris

Pay a visit to this luxurious contemporary chophouse with stylistic nods to Prohibition-era speakeasies. Fantastical dishes include ginger sweet potatoes, veal chops with kumquat-pineapple chutney and live Maine lobster with braised artichokes. Elegant bar with a robust Californian and French wine list. Jackets preferred. Reservations recommended.

🍴 SENSI Map p182
Global Fusion $$$
☎ 877-234-6358; Bellagio, 3600 Las Vegas Blvd S; ⏰ 11am-2:30pm & 5:30-10:30pm; Ⓜ Bally's & Paris; Ⓥ

At this beautiful spot tucked inside the spa tower, the minimalist architecture complements a harmonious menu of seafood and pastas showing Asian and Italian influences. The fantastic sorbets, gelatos and chocolate confections of Jean-Phillipe Patisserie are just around the corner, next to the world's tallest chocolate fountain.

🍴 CAESARS PALACE & FORUM SHOPS
Make reservations for dining with the gods at www.caesarspalace.com, or call ☎ 877-346-4642.

Wolfgang Puck's Spago ($$) is inside the Forum Shops.

🍴 BRADLEY OGDEN Map p182
New American $$$$
☎ 877-346-4642; www.larkcreek.com/bolv; opposite Colosseum, Caesars Palace, 3570 Las Vegas Blvd S; ⏰ 5-11pm; Ⓜ Flamingo/Caesars Palace

With gourmet farm-fresh fare, this San Francisco Bay area chef's restaurant delivers nouveau takes on American classics, such as blue-cheese soufflés and steamed Alaskan halibut with basil vinaigrette. Torch lights and waterfalls demarcate a soothing space. Reservations strongly recommended.

🍴 CHINOIS Map p182
Chinese Fusion $$$
☎ 737-9700; www.wolfgangpuck.com; Forum Shops, Caesars Palace, 3570 Las Vegas Blvd S; ⏰ 11am-10pm Sun-Thu, to 11pm Fri & Sat; Ⓜ Flamingo/Caesars Palace; Ⓥ

Peripatetic chef Wolfgang Puck scores again with his signature Eurasian fusion served in a chic, artistic Far East atmosphere. Pair the firecracker shrimp with a premium cold sake. Happy hour 5pm to 7pm Sunday to Friday.

🍴 CYPRESS STREET MARKETPLACE Map p182
Fast Food $
☎ 731-7110; opposite Colosseum, Caesars Palace, 3570 Las Vegas Blvd S;

⊙ 11am-11pm; Ⓜ Flamingo/Caesars Palace; ⛾ Ⓥ
You can handily charge fresh, made-to-order salads, global wraps, Asian stir-fries, southern barbecue and pizza, along with beer, wine and health drinks, to a 'smart' card, then pay upon exiting. Courtyard tables perch over the casino floor.

🍴 MESA GRILL Map p182
Southwestern $$$
☎ 877-346-4642; http://bobbyflay.com; opposite Colosseum, Caesars Palace, 3570 Las Vegas Blvd S; ⊙ 11am-2:30pm Mon-Fri, 10:30am-3pm Sat & Sun, 5-11pm daily; Ⓜ Flamingo/Caesars Palace; Ⓥ
While the star New York chef doesn't cook on the premises, his bold signature menu of Southwestern fusion fare lives up to the hype, whether it's a sweet potato tamale with crushed pecan butter, blue corn pancakes or spice-rubbed pork tenderloin.

🍴 RESTAURANT GUY SAVOY
Map p182 *Modern French* $$$$
☎ 877-346-4642; www.guysavoy.com; 2nd fl, Augustus Tower, Caesars Palace, 3570 Las Vegas Blvd S; ⊙ 5-10:30pm Wed-Sun; Ⓜ Flamingo/Caesars Palace
With windows overlooking the Roman Plaza outside Caesars Palace, this intimate dining room is the only US outpost of three-star Michelin chef Guy Savoy. Both the culinary concepts and the prices reach heavenly heights. Dare to cut into the spiced sea bass or ladle the artichoke black-truffle soup. Jacket and tie required. Reservations essential but difficult.

Mesa Grill, Caesars Palace

SEE | SHOP | EAT | PLAY

EAT

 FASHION SHOW MALL

¶¶ CAFE BA-BA-REEBA! Map p180

Spanish Tapas $$

☎ 258-1211; www.cafebabareeba.com; street level, Fashion Show Mall, 3200 Las Vegas Blvd S; ⏱ 11:30am-11pm Sun-Thu, to midnight Fri & Sat; 🚌 The Deuce

Inside this bar-bistro, attentive staff present paellas for two and a parade of hot and cold authentic tapas such as *patatas aioli* (garlic potatoes), spicy *gambas* (shrimp) and imported cheeses. Uniquely flavored sangrias and bite-sized desserts tempt you to linger.

¶¶ CAPITAL GRILLE Map p180

Steakhouse $$$

☎ 932-6631; www.thecapitalgrille. com; 3rd fl, Fashion Show Mall, 3200 Las Vegas Blvd S; ⏱ 11:30am-3pm Mon-Fri, noon-3pm Sat, 5-11pm Mon-Sat, 4-10pm Sun; 🚌 The Deuce

What sets this clubby chain steakhouse apart is hand-cut, dry-aged beef, carved chops and succulent seafood. For a posh power lunch, fork into a tenderloin Caesar salad or lobster-crab burger. The Old and New World wine list gets the nod from *Wine Spectator*.

¶¶ MANDALAY BAY & MANDALAY PLACE

For table reservations, click to www.mandalaybay.com or call ☎ 877-632-7800.

¶¶ AUREOLE Map p182

New American $$$$

☎ 632-7401; www.aureolelv.com; Mandalay Bay, 3950 Las Vegas Blvd S; ⏱ 6-10pm, wine-tower lounge 6pm-midnight; 🚌 The Deuce

Chef Charlie Palmer's inspired seasonal American dishes such as oven-roasted pheasant with sweet-potato gnocchi soar to new heights. The chef's tasting menus (from $95) are pure art and it's worth ordering wine just to watch catsuit-clad 'wine angels' ascend the four-story tower. Extensive wine list, formal dress. Reservations essential but difficult.

¶¶ BURGER BAR Map p182

Comfort Food $$

☎ 632-9364; www.fleurdelyssf.com; Mandalay Place, 3930 Las Vegas Blvd S; ⏱ 10:30am-11pm Sun-Thu, to 1am Fri & Sat; 🚌 The Deuce; ♿

Since when is a hamburger worth $60? When it's built with Kobe beef, sautéed foie gras, shaved truffles and Madeira sauce. Chef Hubert Keller (of famed Fleur de Lys) serves up his signature Rossini burger, build-your-own burgers (veggie OK), whimsical desserts and other off-the-cuff gourmet treats.

¶¶ CHARLIE PALMER STEAK

Map p182 *Steakhouse* $$$$

☎ 632-5120; www.charliepalmer.com; lower level, Four Seasons Hotel,

TOP 10 STEAKHOUSES

Vegas has hundreds of places to get a hunk of burnin' red meat. Props go to:

Binion's Ranch Steakhouse (p108) Real cowboys, plus killer views.
Charlie Palmer Steak (opposite) Impeccable service, Mediterranean décor.
Craftsteak (p98) An unusual surf-and-turf menu.
Delmonico Steakhouse (Venetian, p105) Emeril Lagasse's cajun twists.
Envy (p110) Inventive side dishes and sleek design.
Triple George Grill (p110) The city's elite reign here.
N9NE (p115) Champagne, caviar and Chicago style.
Prime Steakhouse (p94) Creative fusion dishes, gilt chandeliers and velvet curtains.
Pullman Bar & Grille (p109) Antiques and a unique cigar lounge.
SW Steakhouse (p107) Exquisite French-influenced fare.

Mandalay Bay, 3960 Las Vegas Blvd S;
🕑 5-10:30pm, lounge to midnight;
🚌 The Deuce

Artisan-aged beef is grilled to perfection at this classy, Spanish-influenced hideaway. Starring on a regional American menu are Kansas City rib eye and Hudson Valley foie gras. Impressive wine list; business casual dress. Reservations essential.

🍽 FLEUR DE LYS Map p182

Modern French $$$$

☎ 632-9400; www.fleurdelyssf.com;
Mandalay Bay, 3950 Las Vegas Blvd S;
🕑 5:30-10:30pm; 🚌 The Deuce

Overseen by French chef Hubert Keller of San Francisco's famous Fleur de Lys, this is a soaring space outfitted with European linens and flower-patterned china, with seasonal tasting menus. Expect flawless service and expert cuisine such as filet mignon with braised oxtail tortellini or Hawaiian swordfish with fennel rouille (there are imaginative vegetarian options on offer as well). Reservations are recommended.

🍽 RED SQUARE Map p182

Modern Russian $$$

☎ 632-7407; Mandalay Bay, 3960 Las Vegas Blvd S; 🕑 5-11pm, bar to 2am;
🚌 The Deuce

How post-perestroika: propaganda art hangs on the walls and the velvety Russian tearoom atmosphere is intoxicating. Comrades here have got rubles to spare for exquisite chicken Kiev, salmon *kulebyaka* or clams topped with caviar. The vodka bar (see the boxed text, p121) is made of solid ice.

EAT | PLAY

EAT

RM Map p182 *Seafood* $$$
☎ 632-9300; www.rmseafood.com;
Mandalay Place, 3930 Las Vegas Blvd S;
🕙 restaurant 5-10:30pm, café 5-11pm
Sun-Thu, to midnight Fri & Sat; 🚌 The
Deuce; 🚻

New York chef Rick Moonen presents the catch of the day. American seafood dishes, such as cajun popcorn and Maine lobster, come with suggested beer pairings and a cornucopia of comfort-food sides like gourmet mac-and-cheese. The downstairs café offers a stripped-down menu, raw bar and 'biscuit bar' serving seafood salads.

🍽 MGM GRAND

Other delectable options include Diego ($$) for margaritas and modern Mexican; sleek Fiamma Trattoria & Bar ($$$) for modish Italian; and polished Pearl ($$$) for Chinese. For reservations, click to www.mgmgrand.com or call ☎ 877-793-7111.

🍽 CRAFTSTEAK Map p182
Steakhouse/Seafood $$$$
☎ 891-7318; www.craftrestaurant.com;
Studio Walk, MGM Grand, 3799 Las Vegas
Blvd S; 🕙 5:30-10:30pm; Ⓜ MGM Grand

From James Beard Award–winning chef Tom Colicchio, this contemporary, richly wood-laden space may lack exclusivity, but makes up

for that with an intriguing menu of grass-fed vs grain-fed strip steaks, and bounty from the sea: regional American oysters, Beluga caviar and Australian lobster tail. Three-course tasting menu from $90.

🍽 EMERIL'S Map p182
Cajun/Creole Seafood $$$
☎ 891-7374; www.emerils.com; Studio
Walk, MGM Grand, 3799 Las Vegas Blvd S;
🕙 11am-2:30pm & 5:30-10:30pm;
Ⓜ MGM Grand

The Crescent City's most televised chef, Emeril Lagasse, cranks it up a notch at his New Orleans fish house, with barbecued oysters and lobster cheesecake. The wine list is an award-winner, and the banana cream pie drizzled with caramel is sumptin' else.

🍽 JOËL ROBUCHON Map p182
Modern French $$$$
☎ 891-7925; www.robuchon.com; MGM
Grand, 3799 Las Vegas Blvd S; 🕙 5:30-
10:30pm Sun-Thu, to 10:30pm Fri & Sat;
Ⓜ MGM Grand

The acclaimed 'Chef of the Century' leads the pack in the French invasion of Las Vegas. Adjacent to the high-rollers' gaming area, the Mansion, Robuchon's plush dining rooms done up in leather and velvet, feel like 1930s Paris. Complex seasonal tasting menus ($225 to $360). Reservations essential but difficult. At next-door L'Atelier de

Joël Robuchon ($$$$) bar seats front an exhibition kitchen.

🍴 SEABLUE Map p182
Seafood $$$

☎ 891-3486; www.michaelmina.net; Bellagio, 3600 Las Vegas Blvd S; ⏲ 5:30-10:30pm; Ⓜ MGM Grand

For impeccably fresh seafood, don't miss Michael Mina's newest creation. Anything from Nantucket Bay scallops to Kumamoto oysters comes raw, fried, steamed and roasted out of two exhibition kitchens. Mix-and-match salads fulfill any whim. Bar seating available.

🍴 SHIBUYA Map p182
Japanese Fusion $$$$

☎ 891-3001; Studio Walk, MGM Grand, 3799 Las Vegas Blvd S; ⏲ 5-10pm Sun-Thu, to 10:30pm Fri & Sat; Ⓜ MGM Grand

A stellar sake cellar, dramatic art spreading behind the sushi bar and tastebud-awakening hot and cold appetizers, such as seaweed dressed up in orange *ponzu* sauce, Kumamoto oysters spiked with green apple tang or snapper ceviche with lemon-lime and white soy delight. *Teppanyaki* grill set menus come with lobster miso soup, plus a sampling of desserts.

🍴 WICHCRAFT Map p182
Deli $

☎ 891-3166; Studio Walk, MGM Grand, 3799 Las Vegas Blvd S; ⏲ 10am-6pm; Ⓜ MGM Grand; ♿ Ⓥ

This airy, bewitching kitchen serves belly-warming sandwiches such as grilled cheddar with smoked ham and baked apples or Sicilian tuna with black olives on a baguette. Perfect side salads of chickpeas, mustard potatoes or fresh fruit are uplifting, as are the s'mores desserts.

🍴 WOLFGANG PUCK BAR & GRILL Map p182 *Cal-Italian* $$

☎ 891-3000; www.wolfgangpuck. com; MGM Grand, 3799 Las Vegas Blvd S; ⏲ 11:30am-10:30pm Sun-Thu, to 11:30pm Fri & Sat; Ⓜ MGM Grand; Ⓥ

California flair pervades this bistro overseeing the casino floor. Truffled potato chips with blue cheese, skirt steak skewers, wood-fired pizzas and ricotta gnocchi in an ultra-contemporary setting

Wolfgang Puck Bar & Grill, MGM Grand

are as thrilling as the New World wine list.

 MIRAGE

Other savory options include the buffet Cravings ($$) and Stack ($$$), the lookalike of Fix (p92). For reservations, click to www.mirage.com or call ☎ 866-339-4566.

🍴 **FIN** Map p180
Contemporary Chinese $$$
☎ 791-7111; Mirage, 3400 Las Vegas Blvd S; 🕑 11am-2:30pm & 5-11pm; 🚌 The Deuce
Elegant yet edgy, this expansive modern dining room wrapped in silk screens and whimsical blue-crystal bubble mobiles spans the spectrum from classic to creative Chinese cuisine, with every dish a tangy winner. After you hit the jackpot, order the braised whole abalone.

🍴 **JAPONAIS** Map p180
Contemporary Japanese $$$
☎ 791-7111; www.japonaislasvegas.com; Mirage, 3400 Las Vegas Blvd S; 🕑 5-11pm Sun-Wed, to 11:30pm Thu-Sat; 🚌 The Deuce
Not another pan-Asian fusion restaurant, you're thinking, right? But with a sexy Jeffrey Beers design and rock-solid Japanese chefs behind the sushi bar, don't worry – you're in good hands. Savor

Japonais, Mirage

playful dishes such as 'The Rock' (NY strip steak sizzling on a hot rock) or 'Tokyo Drums' (teriyaki chicken drumsticks with roasted scallion dipping sauce).

 MONTE CARLO

MONTE CARLO PUB & BREWERY Map p182

Pub Grub $-$$

☎ 730-7777; www.montecarlo.com; Street of Dreams, Monte Carlo, 3770 Las Vegas Blvd S; ☽ bar 11am-3am Sun-Thu, to 4am Fri & Sat, kitchen closes 10pm Sun-Thu, 11pm Fri & Sat; 🚌 The Deuce; Ⓥ
This industrial-size microbrewery with big copper brewing vats fills up after sundown. Kick back with a Silver State Stout and do your best imitation of a couch potato while you glue your eyes to three dozen TVs, all tuned to sports.

 NEW YORK-NEW YORK

Other delicious options include upscale country Irish cooking at Nine Fine Irishmen ($$); Chinese dim sum at Chin Chin Cafe ($-$$); and upstairs Nathan's Famous Hot Dogs ($), New York Pretzel stands ($) and Schrafft's Ice Cream ($) serving 99¢ coffee.

IL FORNAIO Map p182

Northern Italian $$

☎ 740-6403; www.ilfornaio.com; New York-New York, 3790 Las Vegas Blvd S;

☽ 7:30-10:30am & 11:30am-midnight Sun-Thu, to 1am Fri & Sat; Ⓜ MGM Grand; 🚹 Ⓥ
Feast on wood-fired pizzas, seasonal salads and pastas, or make a meal of the antipasti platter with scallops wrapped in pancetta, baked eggplant, truffled cheeses and more (per person $12). Delectable, fresh-baked breakfast goodies such as lemon-pecan scones and hazelnut pastries are also available at Il Fornaio Paneterria (☽ 6am-7:30pm), near the hotel lobby.

VILLAGE EATERIES Map p182

Fast Food $$

☎ 740-6969; www.nynyhotelcasino .com; New York-New York, 3790 Las Vegas Blvd S; ☽ daily; Ⓜ MGM Grand; 🚹 Ⓥ
The cobblestone streets of NY-NY's ersatz Greenwich Village are just bursting with incredibly tasty, wallet-saving options: Greenberg & Sons Deli, authentic down to the egg cream soda; Fulton's Fish Frye for fresh fish and chips; gourmet Jodi Maroni's Sausage Kingdom, straight from Venice Beach; and Gonzalez Y Gonzalez, a traditional tequila-soaked Tex Mex cantina.

 PARIS-LAS VEGAS

With a Cordon Bleu–trained culinary staff of 500, other good options are 24-hour Le Café Île St

Louis ($); pastries at JJ's Boulangerie ($); the Rue de la Paix's La Creperie ($); and Napoleon's (p121) happy-hour carving station.

🍽 EIFFEL TOWER RESTAURANT Map p182
Modern French $$$

☎ 948-6937; www.eiffeltowerrestaurant.com; Eiffel Tower, Paris-Las Vegas, 3655 Las Vegas Blvd S; 🕙 11am-3:30pm & 5-10pm Sun-Thu, to 11:30pm Fri & Sat; Ⓜ Bally's & Paris

The adage about 'the better the view, the worse the food' doesn't apply here. Views of the Strip and Bellagio's fountains are as breathtaking as the near-perfect contemporary renditions of haute classics like foie gras. The chef's tasting menu is recommended, as is the Francophile wine list. Reservations necessary.

🍽 LE VILLAGE BUFFET Map p182
French/Seafood $$

☎ 946-7000; www.parislasvegas.com; Rue de la Paix, Paris-Las Vegas, 3655 Las Vegas Blvd S; 🕙 7am-10pm; Ⓜ Bally's & Paris; ♿ Ⓥ

Fresh fruit and cheeses, cracked crab legs and a wide range of breads and pastries make this arguably the best-value buffet on the Strip. France's various regions are represented at distinct cooking stations. Breakfasts are *magnifique*, especially the Sunday champagne brunch. Expect to queue.

VICTUALS WITH A VIEW

When the panorama is important and price is not, ascend to Alizé (p113), Eiffel Tower Restaurant (left), Binion's Ranch Steakhouse (p108) or Top of the World (opposite). For more down-to-earth romantic vistas, head to Mon Ami Gabi (below) or any of the Bellagio's (p92) lakefront restaurants or Wynn's (p106) lagoon-view restaurants.

🍽 MON AMI GABI Map p182
French/Seafood $$

☎ 944-4224; www.monamigabilasvegas.com; Paris-Las Vegas, 3655 Las Vegas Blvd S; 🕙 11:30am-3pm & 5-11pm Sun-Thu, to midnight Fri & Sat; Ⓜ Bally's & Paris; ♿ Ⓥ

Think *trés* charming Champs Élysées bistro. First-come, first-served outdoor patio tables in the shadow of the Eiffel Tower are almost the only Stripside alfresco dining, *parfait* for people-watching. There's a raw seafood bar, classic steak frites and bountiful vegetarian crepes, quiches and salads. Respectable, reasonable wine list.

🍽 PLANET HOLLYWOOD & MIRACLE MILE SHOPS
🍽 COMMANDER'S PALACE
Map p182 *Cajun/Creole* $$$

☎ 892-8272; www.commanderspalace.com; Miracle Mile Shops, 3663 Las

Vegas Blvd S; 🕒 11:30am-2pm Mon-Fri, 10:30am-2pm Sat & Sun, 5:30-10pm daily; 🚌 The Deuce
Not quite the same as the 19th-century N'awlins original, but it's close. Rest assured that the hospitable Brennan family has put turtle soup au sherry, pecan-crusted catfish and shrimp *rémoulade* on the menu. A live Dixieland jazz band plays during Sunday brunch, and 25¢ martini weekday lunch specials are unbeatable.

🍴 TODAI Map p182
Asian Seafood $$
☎ 892-0021; www.todai.com; Miracle Mile Shops, 3663 Las Vegas Blvd S, enter off Harmon Ave; 🕒 11:30am-2:30pm & 5:30-9:30pm Mon-Thu, to 10pm Fri-Sun; 🚌 The Deuce; 🚻
Inside a shopping mall (p81), this magnificent all-you-can-gorge 160ft (49m) spread of Japanese, Chinese and Korean fare features 15 salads and 40 types of sushi. Lobster, shellfish and crab legs are added to the mix at dinnertime. Desserts rock.

🍴 STRATOSPHERE

🍴 ROXY'S DINER Map p180
Comfort Food $
☎ 380-7777; www.stratospherehotel.com; Stratosphere, 2000 Las Vegas Blvd S; 🕒 11am-10pm Sun-Tue, to 11pm Fri & Sat; 🚌 The Deuce; 🚻 V

In Vegas, everyone has a gimmick. At this '50s-style diner, servers do a little song-and-dance number straight out of *Grease* every 15 minutes. It's hilarious fun, but it sure does slow service down. Big blue-plate specials won't leave you hungry.

🍴 TOP OF THE WORLD Map p180
Continental $$$$
☎ 380-7711; www.stratospherehotel.com; Stratosphere, 2000 Las Vegas Blvd S; 🕒 11am-3pm & 5:30-10:30pm Sun-Thu, to 11pm Fri & Sat; 🚌 The Deuce
A dressy, revolving romantic roost perched atop the Stratosphere Tower (p70). While taking in the cloud-level views, patrons enjoy impeccable service and delicious (if overpriced) mains such as Colorado rack of lamb and Dover sole. Reservations recommended for lunch, required for dinner. Excellent wine list.

🍴 TI (TREASURE ISLAND)

For reservations, visit www.treasureisland.com or call ☎ 894-7111. Dishes ($$) is among the Strip's interesting buffets.

🍴 CANTER'S DELI Map p180
Jewish Deli $-$$
☎ 894-7370; www.cantersdeli.com; TI (Treasure Island), 3300 Las Vegas Blvd S; 🕒 11am-midnight Mon-Fri, from 9am Sat & Sun; 🚌 The Deuce

What did Canter's import from their landmark LA delicatessen? You guessed it: their infamously gruff service. Steal one of the seats at the stainless-steel counter or a super-mod booth and settle back to taste authentic deli fare that's as good as it gets.

🍴 ISLA MEXICAN KITCHEN & TEQUILA BAR Map p180
Mexican/Southwestern $$

☎ 894-7111; TI (Treasure Island), 3300 Las Vegas Blvd S; 🕙 4-11pm, to midnight Sun-Tue & Thu, bar 11am-2am daily; 🚌 The Deuce

Modern art enlivens the walls of this invention by Mexican-born chef Richard Sandoval, serving a fusion of south-of-the-border tastes. Be forewarned: plates are apportioned for giants. Calling on Isla's tequila goddess to help decipher the bounteous menu of agave elixirs is a must.

🍴 PHO AT THE COFFEE SHOP
Map p180 *Vietnamese* $-$$

☎ 894-7111; TI (Treasure Island), 3300 Las Vegas Blvd S; 🕙 11am-midnight Sun-Thu, to 3am Fri & Sat; 🚌 The Deuce; 👶

Around the side of TI's 24-hour coffee shop, dash inside and away from the slot machines to slurp Vietnamese noodle soups and more. It's some of the Strip's cheapest, most authentic Asian fare.

🍴 SOCIAL HOUSE Map p180
Sushi/Pan-Asian $$$

☎ 894-7223; www.socialhouselv.com; TI (Treasure Island), 3300 Las Vegas Blvd S;

Social House, TI (Treasure Island)

⊙ 5-11pm Sun & Mon, to 4am Tue-Sat;
🚌 The Deuce

Above Tangerine (p130), this trendy sushi and sake bar is designed for socializing. While the panko-crusted crab cakes, lemongrass shrimp and tamarind short ribs may not always hit the right note, the ultramodern setting with shoji-papered windows and a Strip-view patio with bonsai trees do.

🍴 VENETIAN & GRAND CANAL SHOPPES

This bite of Italy is a world-class dining destination. Reservations (☎ 877-883-6423; www.venetian .com) and formal dress are a must for the fancier places. For a chic scene, dine at Tao Asian Bistro ($$$) downstairs from Tao night-club (p132).

🍴 BOUCHON Map p180
French/Seafood $$$

☎ 414-6200; www.frenchlaundry.com; Venezia Tower, Venetian, 3355 Las Vegas Blvd S; ⊙ 7-10:30am & 5-11pm daily, 11:30am-2:30pm Sat & Sun, oyster bar & cocktail lounge 3pm-midnight; Ⓜ Harrah's/Imperial Palace

Napa Valley wunderkind Thomas Keller's new rendition of a Lyon-naise bistro features an award-winning menu of seasonal classics. The poolside setting complements the oyster bar, extensive raw sea-food selection, super wine list and

decadent breakfasts and desserts. Reservations recommended.

🍴 CANALETTO Map p180
Northern Italian $$$

☎ 733-0070; Venetian, 3355 Las Vegas Blvd S; ⊙ 11:30am-11pm Sun-Thu, to midnight Fri & Sat; Ⓜ Harrah's/Imperial Palace

A showy exhibition kitchen and sky-high ceilings emphasize the solid northern Italian cooking. To be safe, stick with signature dishes such as porcini risotto and roasted chicken. Aim for a table with a gondola view.

🍴 DELMONICO STEAKHOUSE
Map p180 *Steakhouse* $$$

☎ 414-3737; www.emerils.com; Vene-tian, 3355 Las Vegas Blvd S; ⊙ 11:30am-1:45pm & 5-10pm Sun-Thu, to 10:30pm Fri & Sat; Ⓜ Harrah's/Imperial Palace

Bam! It's celeb chef Emeril La-gasse's greatest gourmet hits, as seen on TV. The cuts are ready for prime time, the influences are Cre-ole and the chateaubriand-for-two is carved tableside. Big oak doors open into a vault-ceilinged space. Reservations essential.

🍴 LUTÈCE Map p180
Modern French $$$

☎ 414-2220; Venetian, 3355 Las Vegas Blvd S; ⊙ 5:30-10:30pm; Ⓜ Harrah's/ Imperial Palace

Impeccable modern renditions of classic gourmet French fare

(like pan-roasted squab with shallot marmalade) are dramatically presented in a sophisticated, austere setting. The wine cellar is top-notch and the superb seafood dishes are as sought-after as canalside seats with Strip views. Reservations essential.

PINOT BRASSERIE Map p180
French-Californian $$$

☎ 414-8888; www.patinagroup.com; Venetian, 3355 Las Vegas Blvd S; ⏲ 7-10am & 11:30am-3pm Mon-Fri, 7am-3pm Sat & Sun, 5:30-10:30pm Sun-Thu, 5:30-11:30pm Fri & Sat; Ⓜ Harrah's/Imperial Palace

The architectural accents and the kitchen's copper pots are authentic French imports. Traditionally, a brasserie (Alsacean for 'brewery') was for beer and the sustenance was cheap. At this star LA import, the focus is purely gourmet. Don't miss the fresh-shucked shellfish and wine-tasting flights.

POSTRIO Map p180
Cal-Italian $$$

☎ 796-1110; www.wolfgangpuck.com; Grand Canal Shoppes, Venetian, 3355 Las Vegas Blvd S; ⏲ 11:30am-10pm; Ⓜ Harrah's/Imperial Palace; ♿ Ⓥ

This offshoot of Wolfgang Puck's San Francisco original features playful signature dishes like the lobster club sandwich. Devotees can't get enough of the creative

pizzas, pastas and rich desserts. The patio is designed for people-watching. Good wine list.

ZEFFIRINO Map p180
Italian $$$

☎ 414-3500; Grand Canal Shoppes, Venetian, 3355 Las Vegas Blvd S; ⏲ 11:30am-midnight; Ⓜ Harrah's/Imperial Palace

Housemade breads and seafood prepared with Venetian techniques, such as lobster risotto with saffron, are the highlights. Hand-crafted furnishings accent the elegant dining room, with porch seating overlooking the canal.

WYNN

Elegant 24-hour Terrace Point Café ($-$$) and Sugar & Ice ($), a café serving pastries and espresso drinks, both front cool patios. Wynn's buffet ($$) rates among the Strip's finest. Reservations (call ☎ 248-3463, 888-353-3463, or visit www.wynnlasvegas.com) and upscale dress are highly recommended.

ALEX Map p180
French/Mediterranean $$$$

☎ 248-3463; Wynn, 3131 Las Vegas Blvd S; ⏲ 6-10pm Tue-Sun; 🚌 The Deuce

Beloved, legendary chef Alessandro Stratta stretches his wings at this five-star French restaurant, with wildly successful high-concept dishes such as risotto with crisp chicken oysters or herb-crusted rack of lamb with basil chutney and chickpea crepe. The pastry chef's dessert creations are not to be skipped. Jackets suggested for men.

🍴 BARTOLOTTA RISTORANTE DI MARE Map p180
Italian Seafood $$$-$$$$

☎ 770-3305; Wynn, 3131 Las Vegas Blvd S; ⏲ 5:30-10:30pm; 🚌 The Deuce
Yet another of Wynn's stable of James Beard Award winners, chef Paul Bartolotta interprets fresh seafood flown in daily from Europe in a Mediterranean style, along with fresh-made pastas. The spiny lobster *all'acqua pazza* (literally, 'crazy water') is a signature dish.

🍴 DANIEL BOULUD BRASSERIE Map p180
Modern French $$$

☎ 770-3310; www.danielnyc.com; Wynn, 3131 Las Vegas Blvd S; ⏲ 5:30-10:30pm; 🚌 The Deuce
From the chef who birthed NYC's Daniel restaurant, this is where carnivores should head for gourmet burgers stuffed with foie gras and black truffles, bacon-crusted pork chops and Maine lobster salads with curry-lime vinaigrette, as well as tamer platters of French brasserie classics to be shared.

🍴 OKADA Map p180
Japanese Fusion $$-$$$

☎ 770-3320; Wynn, 3131 Las Vegas Blvd S; ⏲ 5:30-10:30pm Sun-Thu, to 11:30pm Fri & Sat; 🚌 The Deuce
At this sushi bar, *robatayaki* and *teppanyaki* grill overlooking the lagoon and a bonsai-sized Japanese garden, chef Masa Ishizawa exhibits masterful Eurasian twists on Japanese classics, like red miso bouillabaisse or braised short ribs with quail eggs.

🍴 RED 8 ASIAN BISTRO Map p180
Pan-Asian $$

☎ 770-3380; Wynn, 3131 Las Vegas Blvd S; ⏲ 11am-11pm Sun-Thu, to 1am Fri & Sat; 🚌 The Deuce
A bustling spot just off the main casino floor, where the action never stops. People line up for satay dishes of roast chicken and beef, bowls of steaming hot curry noodles and pan-Asian barbecue, all from the vivid mind of Malaysian chef Hisham Johari.

🍴 SW STEAKHOUSE Map p180
Steakhouse $$$$

☎ 248-3463; Wynn, 3131 Las Vegas Blvd S; ⏲ 5:30-10:30pm; 🚌 The Deuce
This high-roller's chic chophouse does exquisite renditions of such old-school classics as Bartlett pear salads, lobster bouillabaisse and filet thermidor, but it's the prime cuts of steak that some rave are

the best in town. An open-air patio overlooks the lagoon.

🍴 TABLEAU Map p180
New American $$$$

☎ 248-3463; Tower Suites, Wynn, 3131 Las Vegas Blvd S; ☽ 8-10:30am Mon-Sat, 11:30am-2:30pm & 5:30-10pm daily; 🚌 The Deuce

Feel like a VIP inside Wynn's ivory tower and experience the French-influenced stylings of chef Mark LoRusso, a meteorically rising Vegas star. The biggest payoff is at breakfast, featuring everything from peach ricotta pancakes to poached eggs with duck hash and citrus hollandaise sauce. At dinner the chef's seven-course seasonal tasting menu ($115) comes with a superb vegetarian option ($85).

DOWNTOWN & NAKED CITY

🍴 BINION'S RANCH STEAKHOUSE Map pp184-5
Steakhouse $$$

☎ 382-1600, 800-937-6537; www .binions.com; Binion's, 128 E Fremont St; ☽ 5-11pm; 🚌 The Deuce

When high rollers finish up in the poker room, they retire their Stetsons and ride the glass elevator up to this classy old Vegas penthouse meatery for stunning 24th-floor views and fine feasts of juicy chops with all the old-school fix-in's. Reservations recommended.

🍴 FLORIDA CAFÉ Map pp186-7
Cuban $$

☎ 385-3013; www.floridacafecuban .com; 1401 Las Vegas Blvd S; ☽ 7am-10pm; 🚌 The Deuce; ♿

The hub of Naked City's Cuban community is advertised on bus stops all over town, but don't let that dissuade you. Island artworks hang on the walls and a Cuban chef reigns over the kitchen, cooking up shredded steak, hearty fried pork and seasoned chicken with yellow rice. *Café con leche,* flan and *batidos* (tropical shakes) are superb.

🍴 LILLIE'S NOODLE HOUSE
Map pp184-5 *Chinese/Pan-Asian* $$

☎ 385-7111; www.goldennugget .com; Golden Nugget, 129 E Fremont St; ☽ 6pm-midnight Tue-Thu, to 1am Fri & Sat; 🚌 The Deuce; Ⓥ

The imperially rich tapestries, gold-flecked tables and red-and-black tones overwhelm the serviceable Cantonese, Szechuan and pan-Asian cooking, as this dining space is among the most gorgeous in Glitter Gulch. Fusion desserts like ginger crème brûlée are ambrosial.

🍴 LUV-IT FROZEN CUSTARD
Map pp186-7 *Fast Food* $

☎ 384-6452; www.luvitfrozencustard .com; 505 E Oakey Blvd; ☽ 1-10pm Tue-Thu, 1-11pm Fri & Sat, closed Dec; 🚌 The Deuce; ♿ Ⓥ

A mecca for locals since 1973, Luv-It has handmade custard concoctions that are way creamier than ice cream. Flavors change daily, so you'll be tempted to go back. Try a 'Luv Stick' custard bar, thick milkshake or sundae piled higher than Everest.

MAHALO EXPRESS

Map pp184-5 *Hawaiian Fast Food* $
☎ 385-1664; www.vegasclubcasino.net; Vegas Club, 18 E Fremont St; ⏰ 6:30am-9:30pm; 🚌 The Deuce; ♿

The truest tastes of the islands are found at this cafeteria. Your fellow diners are likely to be homesick Hawaiian families or bleary-eyed gamblers who know there's nothing like a mixed plate of two-scoop rice, macaroni salad and succulent meat to stave off a hangover. Walk over to the Cal casino hotel afterward for Lappert's Hawaii-style ice cream.

MERMAIDS Map pp184-5
Fast Food $
☎ 382-5777; 32 E Fremont St; ⏰ 24hr; 🚌 The Deuce

Hook a strand of Mardi Gras beads at the door, then weave your way past the rabid slot jockeys to the back counter for outrageous deep-fried Twinkies and Oreos snowed under by powdered sugar. So sinfully tasty.

PULLMAN BAR & GRILLE

Map pp184-5 *Steakhouse* $$$
☎ 387-1896; www.mainstreetcasino .com; Main Street Station, 200 N Main St; ⏰ 5-10pm Wed-Sun, to 10:30pm Fri & Sat; 🚌 The Deuce

A well-kept secret, the clubby Pullman features the finest Black Angus beef and Pacific Rim seafood specialties, along with a good wine list. Dine amid gorgeous carved wood paneling and a fortune's worth of antiques. The centerpiece namesake is a 1926 Pullman train car, now a cigar lounge where suited-up patrons quaff a brandy after dinner. Reservations recommended.

REDWOOD BAR & GRILLE

Map pp184-5 *Steakhouse* $$
☎ 385-1222, www.thecal.com; California, 12 E Ogden Ave; ⏰ 5:30-11pm Fri-Tue; 🚌 The Deuce

The Cal's friendly steakhouse is infused with aloha spirit. Although the porterhouse special ($18) isn't on the menu, it's available for the asking and has as its grand finale a plump apple dumpling in cinnamon-raisin sauce.

SAN FRANCISCO SHRIMP BAR & DELI Map pp184-5
American Seafood $
☎ 385-1906; www.goldengatecasino .com; Golden Gate, 1 E Fremont St; ⏰ 24hr; 🚌 The Deuce; ♿

AFTER HOURS

Late-night meal deals come and go, but the following are hard to beat: Mr Lucky's at the Hard Rock (p56) does an unlisted 24/7 surf-and-turf special ($7.77); **Ellis Island Casino & Brewery** (☎ 733-8901; www.ellisislandcasino.com; 4187 Koval Lane) offers a full 10oz steak dinner ($5.95) around the clock; and Binion's (p45) coffee shop has a 10oz New York strip ($4.99) from 11pm to 7am. Other good late-night dining bets include Firefly (opposite), Pho at the Coffee Shop (p104), Lillie's Noodle House (p108), Ping Pang Pong (p115), In-N-Out Burger (p114) and Metro Pizza (opposite).

The best 99¢ shrimp cocktail in town (it's tiny – supersize it for $2.99) is the draw inside downtown's historic San Francisco–themed hotel. For the low-rollers' surf-and-turf special, veer across the street to Binion's snack bar (open to midnight on weekends) for an old-fashioned butcher-shop burger.

🍴 SECOND STREET GRILL
Map pp184-5
Steakhouse/Seafood $$$
☎ 385-3232; www.fremontcasino.com; Fremont, 200 E Fremont St; ⏰ 6-10pm Thu-Sun, to 11pm Fri & Sat; 🚌 The Deuce
At this art-deco downtown hideaway, which thankfully not many tourists know about, the chef flies

in seafood fresh from Hawaii. Red-meat lovers can get a steak with all the trimmings. Bring the love of your life, and dine like retro royalty.

🍴 TRIPLE GEORGE GRILL
Map pp184-5
Steakhouse/Seafood $$$
☎ 384-2761; www.triplegeorgegrill.com; 201 N 3rd St; ⏰ 11am-10pm Mon-Thu, 11am-11pm Fri, 3-11pm Sat; 🚌 The Deuce
A wildly successful import from the San Francisco Bay area, it's bow is the haunt of the city's movers and shakers, not only for its dry-aged steaks and classic seafood dishes, but also its Rat Pack–worthy cocktails and rare wines also poured at sidebar (see the boxed text, p121).

UNLV & EASTSIDE
🍴 ENVY Map pp190-1
Steakhouse $$$$
☎ 784-5716; www.envysteakhouse.com; Renaissance, 3400 Paradise Rd; ⏰ 11am-2:30pm daily, 5-10pm Sun-Thu, 5-10:30pm Fri & Sat; Ⓜ Convention Center
Envy's name is no lie. A dramatic mod entrance leads inside to where powerbrokers recline against high-backed chairs amid a boldly splashed color palette of paints and hanging lanterns. Both the steak and seafood get high marks, along with inventive side dishes like truffle *reggiano*

fries. Smart wine list. Reservations recommended.

▯↑ FIREFLY Map pp190-1
Tapas/Fusion $$
☎ 369-3971; www.fireflylv.com;
Citibank Plaza, 3900 Paradise Rd;
🕒 11:30am-2am Mon-Thu, 11:30am-3am Fri, 5pm-3am Sat, 5pm-2am Sun;
🚌 108

Firefly is always packed. Folks are venturing off-Strip not just for the late-night patio scene, but also for the food. Spain shakes hands with Asia, as chorizo clams jostle alongside shrimp potstickers in a mustard-sesame glaze. A backlit bar dispenses sangria and lychee-infused vodka. On some lucky nights, hot Latin turntablists spin.

▯↑ LOTUS OF SIAM Map pp190-1
Thai $$
☎ 735-3033; www.saipinchutima.com;
Commercial Center, 953 E Sahara Ave;
🕒 11:30am-2:30pm Mon-Fri, 5:30-9:30pm Mon-Thu, 5:30-10pm Fri-Sun; 🚌 204; **V**

The most authentic Thai kitchen this side of Chiang Mai. The menu includes both Isaan and Northern Thai specialties like savory *larb* salads with sticky rice. Ignore the strip-mall location while you concentrate on fresh flavors bursting out of your bowl. Award-winning German and American wine list.

▯↑ METRO PIZZA Map pp190-1
Pizza $
☎ 736-1955; www.metropizza.com; 1395 E Tropicana Ave; 🕒 11am-10pm Sun-Thu, to 11pm Fri & Sat; 🚌 201; 🚼 **V**

Firefly, Citibank Plaza

If you don't make it all the way out here to taste Vegas' best thin-crust pie, you can still devour a cheesy slice at Metro's outpost inside 24-hour **Ellis Island Casino & Brewery** (☎ 733-8901; 4178 Koval Lane) east of the Strip.

🍴 NOBU Map pp190-1

Japanese Fusion $$$

☎ 693-5090; www.hardrockhotel.com; **Hard Rock, 4455 Paradise Rd;** ⏲ 6-11pm; 🚌 108, 202

Iron Chef Matasuhisa's sequel to his NYC namesake is almost as good as the original. The beats are down-tempo, the setting pure Zen. Stick to the namesake classics, such as black cod with miso, and imaginative desserts and cocktails. Feeling flush: try the chef's special *omakase* dinner (from $100). Reservations recommended.

🍴 ORIGIN INDIA Map pp190-1

Modern Indian $$

☎ 734-6342; www.originindiarestaurant.com; 4480 Paradise Rd; ⏲ 11:30am-11:30pm; 🚌 108, 202; V

A gorgeous sunset-colored dining room and epic New World and European wine list are only bonuses. What brings in eagle-eyed feasters is the inventive Indian menu ranging across the subcontinent, featuring royal recipes to modern fusion. Vegetarians will think they've reached nirvana. Lunch specials available till 3pm.

🍴 PAYMON'S MEDITERRANEAN CAFÉ

Map pp190-1 *Mediterranean/Deli* $$

☎ 731-6030; www.paymons.com; 4147 S Maryland Parkway, at Flamingo Rd; ⏲ 11am-1am Mon-Thu, to 3am Fri & Sat, to 5pm Sun; 🚌 202; ♿ V

Nobu, Hard Rock

A fresh find for vegetarian fare such as baked eggplant with fresh garlic, baba ganoush, tabouli and hummus. Carnivores should try the kebab sandwich, gyros salad or savory rotisserie lamb. Adjacent Hookah Lounge (p121) is tranquil.

🍴 PINK TACO Map pp190-1
Mexican $-$$
☎ 693-5000; www.hardrockhotel.com; Hard Rock, 4455 Paradise Rd; ☷ 11am-10pm Sun-Thu, to midnight Fri & Sat; 🚍 108, 202

The *comida* is Californicated but extremely tasty at this Baja fish taco shack crossed with a low rider themed Sunset Strip tequila bar. The margaritas are two-for-one and all the appetizers are half-price during the happening happy hour (4pm to 7pm weekdays).

🍴 SIMON KITCHEN & BAR
Map pp190-1 *Eclectic* $$$
☎ 693-4440; www.hardrockhotel.com; Hard Rock, 4455 Paradise Rd; ☷ 6-10:30pm Sun-Thu, to 11:30pm Fri & Sat; 🚍 108, 202

The newest hard-rockin' option features the eclectic surf-and-turf fare of Kerry Simon, who made an appearance on *Iron Chef* on a Harley. 'Topless' apple pie, colossal crab cakes with papaya slaw, and wasabi mashed potatoes – they may be foodie fads, but the svelte scene puts it over the top.

TOP FIVE NON-CASINO NOSHES
- > Envy (p110)
- > Firefly (p111)
- > Hash House A Go Go (p114)
- > Origin India (opposite)
- > Rosemary's (p115)

WESTSIDE

For adventurous palates, lively Asian restaurants anchor around the ornate Chinese gate on Spring Mountain Rd, where you'll find plenty of Hong Kong and Korean barbecue houses, Vietnamese pho shops, Japanese sushi bars and pan-Asian bubble tea dispensaries.

🍴 ALIZÉ Map pp188-9
French/Continental $$$
☎ 951-7000; www.alizelv.com; 56th fl, Palms, 4321 W Flamingo Rd; ☷ 5:30-10pm Sun-Thu, to 11pm Fri & Sat; 🚍 202

Vegas chef André Rochat's top-drawer gourmet room is named after a gentle Mediterranean trade wind. The panoramic views (enjoyed by nearly every table) are stunning, just like the haute French cuisine. An enormous wine-bottle tower dominates the room. Jacket and tie suggested. Reservations essential.

🍴 CARNIVAL WORLD & VILLAGE SEAFOOD BUFFETS

Map pp188-9 *Buffet/Seafood* $$-$$$
☎ 252-7777; www.playrio.com; Rio, 3700 W Flamingo Rd; 🕑 Carnival World 7am-10pm Mon-Fri, 7:30am-10pm Sat & Sun, Village Seafood 4-10pm Sun-Thu, 3-11pm Fri & Sat; 🚌 free Strip shuttle from Harrah's; ♿

With dishes from China, Brazil, Mexico and Italy on offer, as well as loads of fresh seafood and handmade Italian gelato, some say Carnival World is the best all-around buffet in town. The more expensive Village Seafood Buffet is for those who just can't get enough crab legs, lobster tails and oysters, plus salads, pasta and fresh-baked breads.

🍴 GARDUÑO'S Map pp188-9

Mexican $$
☎ 942-7777; www.palms.com; casino level, Palms, 4321 W Flamingo Rd; 🕑 11am-9:30pm Mon, to 10pm Sun & Tue-Thu, to 11pm Fri & Sat; 🚌 202
While the menu of *combos tradicionales* plays more to the frat-boy palate, there are a few truly authentic tastes to be found, such as the pork *posole*. Tables on the upstairs terrace are best, or just belly up to the Blue Agave oyster and chili bar for shooters and a lip-smacking coconut margarita instead.

🍴 GOLDEN STEER Map p180

Steakhouse $$$
☎ 384-4470; www.goldensteerlv.com; 308 W Sahara Ave; 🕑 11:30am-2:30pm Mon-Fri, 4:30-10:15pm daily; 🚌 204
No, it's not the best steak in town. But that's not at all why you're coming to this deliciously tacky steakhouse with the steer's head out front. This is the same place where the Rat Pack and Elvis dined, so you're here to soak up the vibes and pretend it's 1958 all over again.

🍴 HASH HOUSE A GO GO

Map pp178-9 *Comfort Food* $$
☎ 804-4646; www.hashhouseagogo .com; 6800 W Sahara Ave, east of S Rainbow Blvd; 🕑 7:30am-2:30pm daily, 5-10pm Mon-Sat; 🚌 204; ♿ Ⓥ
Fill up before going to Red Rock Canyon (p146) on this SoCal import's famed 'twisted farm food,' which has to be seen to be believed. The pancakes are as big as tractor tires and the huge egg scrambles and hashes could knock over a cow. Meatloaf, pot pies, chicken-'n'-biscuits and wild boar sloppy joes are what's for dinner.

🍴 IN-N-OUT BURGER

Map pp188-9 *Fast Food* $
☎ 800-786-1000; www.in-n-out.com; 4888 Industrial Rd; 🕑 10:30am-1am Sun-Thu, to 1:30am Fri & Sat; 🚌 202; ♿

At California's famous In-N-Out Burger, where the patties are never frozen and the fries are hand-diced every day, there's a secret menu. Ask for your burger 'animal style' (with mustard, an onion-grilled bun and extra-special sauce).

🍴 N9NE Map pp188-9
Steakhouse $$$
☎ 933-9900; http://n9negroup.com; Palms, 4321 W Flamingo Rd; 🕑 5-11pm Sun-Thu, to 11:30pm Fri & Sat; 🚌 202
The Palms' sizzling steakhouse skews toward 20- and 30-somethings and is a hot spot for celeb sightings. A dramatically lit room centers on the champagne and Russian caviar bar; at tables and booths the Chicago-style aged steaks and chops keep on coming, along with everything else from oysters Rockefeller to sashimi. Reservations recommended.

🍴 PING PANG PONG Map pp188-9
Chinese $$
☎ 367-7111; www.goldcoastcasino .com; Gold Coast, 4000 W Flamingo Rd; 🕑 10am-3pm & 5pm-3am; 🚌 202; ♿
The name's fun to say, isn't it? But let's get serious for a minute. Asian package tourists vote with their feet, and it's always crowded here. Designed by chef Kevin Wu, it has a wok-tossed menu that ranges across the regions of China, from

Cantonese roast chicken to Beijing seafood stew. At lunchtime the Cantonese dim sum is a pleasure. Service is fast and furious.

🍴 ROSEMARY'S Map pp178-9
New American/Cajun $$$
☎ 869-2251; www.rosemarysrestaur ant.com; 8125 W Sahara Ave, west of S Buffalo Dr; 🕑 11:30am-2:30pm Mon-Fri, 5:30-10:30pm daily; 🚌 204; V
Words fail to describe the epicurean ecstasy you'll encounter here. Yes, it's in a strip mall, and it's a long drive from the Strip. But once you bite into such divine offerings as Texas barbecue shrimp with Maytag blue-cheese slaw or grilled pork chops with creole mustard sauce, you'll forget about all that. Wine and beer pairings make each course sublime. Reservations recommended.

🍴 SALT LICK BBQ
Barbecue $-$$
☎ 797-7535; www.redrocklasvegas .com; Red Rock Casino Resort Spa, 11011 W Charleston Blvd, at I 215; 🕑 11am-10pm Mon-Thu, to 11pm Fri-Sun; 🚌 208
Straight from the Lone Star State, this green oak-smoked barbecue house is absolutely the best in town. Chow down on sweetly tender beef brisket, gigantic pork ribs and heaping smoked turkey salads after a hard day on the Red Rock range. Yee-haw!

Michael Jordan
Chef at Rosemary's (p115)

Best thing about being a chef in Las Vegas The diversity of the market, from international clientele to a local community that's strong and sophisticated. **Why you love to cook** Because it makes people happy. **Favorite dishes on the menu** Beef carpaccio with an arugula and Granny Smith apple salad and candied walnuts, and the barbecue shrimp with Maytag blue cheese slaw. **The story behind the great beer pairings at Rosemary's** When I was working with Emeril Lagasse, it was always wine-driven. My general manager Mike Shelby, who I've been friends with since I was 19 years old, turned me on to the great world of beer. We wanted to make a statement right from the start that beer is as dynamic and diversified as the world of wine. **Percentage of local patrons vs tourists here on any given night** 60/40. **Best late-night diner food** Downtown's White Cross drugstore and the Peppermill casino's coffee shop on the Strip (see Fireside Lounge, p120).

🍴 SAZIO Map pp188-9
Italian $$

☎ 948-9500; www.saziolasvegas.com;
Orleans, 4500 W Tropicana Ave;
🕐 11am-4pm & 4-10pm Sun-Thu, to
10:30pm Fri & Sat; 🚌 free Strip shuttle
from Harrah's; ♿ Ⓥ

With whimsical portraits of Vegas
showgirls and stand-up comics,
colorful Sazio (which translates as
'to be satisfied') is a family-friendly
eatery designed by chef Gustave
Mahler. Traditional pastas and
pizzas, as well as creative salads
and focaccia sandwiches, are more
than respectable.

🍴 TABLE 34
New American $$

☎ 263-0034; 600 E Warm Springs Rd,
east of Bermuda Rd; 🕐 11am-3pm Mon-
Fri, 5-10pm Tue-Sat; 🚌 217

If you're killing time before a
flight or starving upon arrival,
detour here just south of McCarran Airport. In-the-know locals
have long been fans of the chef's
seasonal New American cuisine,
evincing haute comfort food and
Italianesque accents. Top-notch
wine bar.

⭐ PLAY

Even if Las Vegas didn't invent the 24/7 lifestyle, it has perfected it. Catch a stage show before midnight, groove to a DJ till dawn, then watch drag racing at noon. This cowtown attracts more than its share of headliners, including celebrity entertainers you thought were dead – whoops! Recently haute culture has blossomed, too.

The Strip is the obvious all-hours hotspot for drinking, spas, shows and clubbing. You can go broke seeing and doing all there is to see and do, but also be entertained for zero money by jaw-dropping spectacles like the Mirage's erupting volcano or the Bellagio's dancing fountains. Las Vegans let loose at hipster haunts on the edges of downtown, university-student hangouts on the Eastside, strip clubs on the industrial Westside and neighborhood bars and casinos in the 'burbs.

Free tabloids *Las Vegas Weekly* (www.lasvegasweekly.com) and *CityLife* (www.lvcitylife.com) hit the streets on Thursday and, when combined with the 'Neon' section of the *Las Vegas Review-Journal* on Friday, offer comprehensive arts and entertainment listings. Many free tourist mags such as *Showbiz Weekly* and *What's On* have encyclopedic listings of shows.

SAME-DAY DISCOUNT TICKETS

Coca-Cola Tickets 2Nite (Map p182; ☎ 888-484-9264; Showcase Mall, 3785 Las Vegas Blvd S; 🕙 noon-9pm) On the South Strip in front of the giant Coca-Cola bottle.

Tix 4 Tonight (☎ 877-849-4868; www.tix4tonight.com) Center Strip (Map p180; in front of Neiman Marcus, Fashion Show Mall, 3200 Las Vegas Blvd S; 🕙 11am-8pm); downtown (Map pp184-5; Four Queens, 202 E Fremont St; 🕙 10am-7pm); North Strip (Map p182; 2955 Las Vegas Blvd S; 🕙 11am-8pm); South Strip (Map p182; Hawaii Marketplace, 3743 Las Vegas Blvd S; 🕙 11am-8pm)

Left Pure (p132), Caesars Palace

SEE | SHOP | EAT | PLAY

PLAY

 BARS

The vast majority of Sin City's watering holes are smoke-filled, and antismoking propositions are viewed with heartfelt disdain by voters. Many bars stay open until 2am or even around-the-clock. Happy hours are usually 4pm till 7pm, with 'graveyard' happy hours after midnight.

⭐ ART BAR Map pp186-7
☎ 437-2787; http://lvartbar.com; 1511 S Main St; admission free; ⌚ 24hr; 🚌 108, 207

Hipsters, intellectuals and other alt-cultural types gravitate toward the sparkly neon atomic burst outside this art gallery. There's a circular bar for meeting the local wildlife, retro sofas for inviting tête-à-têtes and a closet-sized stage for live bands and DJs. Free wi-fi internet access.

⭐ BEAUTY BAR Map pp184-5
☎ 598-1965; www.beautybar.com; 517 E Fremont St; admission $5-10; ⌚ 9pm-2am Sun-Tue, 5pm-2am Wed-Fri, 9pm-4am Sat; 🚌 107

Swill a cocktail, watch the manicure demonstrations or just chill inside the salvaged innards of a 1950s New Jersey beauty salon. DJs rotate nightly, spinning tiki lounge tones to '80s garage rock or funk and soul on 'Badass Fridays.'

⭐ CARNAVAL COURT Map p180
☎ 369-5000; www.harrahs.com; Harrah's, 3475 Las Vegas Blvd S; ⌚ 12:30pm-2am; Ⓜ Harrah's/Imperial Palace

Outside Harrah's, flair bartenders juggle fire before raucous crowds for whom spring break never ended. Live pop bands and DJs tear up the stage at night, but all eyes are on the hot bods at the bar. Party on, dudes.

⭐ ESPN ZONE Map p182
☎ 933-3776; http://espnzone.com; New York-New York, 3790 Las Vegas Blvd S; ⌚ 11am-11pm Mon-Thu, 11am-midnight Fri & Sat, 9am-11pm Sun; Ⓜ MGM Grand

It's a high-tech sports fan's wildest dream come true. 'Zone Throne' viewing stations (reclining chairs with headsets) are installed in front of giant screens, or at booths where you can surf sports online then flip the channel to any televised game. Memorabilia hangs on the walls, and upstairs is a superstar arcade (p69).

⭐ FIRESIDE LOUNGE Map p180
☎ 735-7635; www.peppermilllasvegas.com; Peppermill, 2985 Las Vegas Blvd S; admission free; ⌚ 24hr; 🚌 The Deuce

Don't be blinded by the outlandishly colored neon. The Strip's most spellbinding romantic hideaway awaits inside this retro coffee shop. Courting couples flock here for the sunken fire pit and cozy blue-velvet nooks. Skip the food – sup on a Scorpion.

⭐ HOFBRÄUHAUS Map pp190-1
☎ 853-2337; www.hofbrauhauslasvegas.com; 4510 Paradise Rd; admission free; 🕑 11am-11pm Sun-Thu, to midnight Fri & Sat; 🚌 108, 202

TOP FIVE SPECIALTY BARS
Isla Tequila Bar (Isla Mexican Kitchen, p104) Let the 'tequila goddess' guide you through the wonders of premium agave elixirs.
Nine Fine Irishmen (New York-New York, p49) Stout Irish beers, rare whiskies and other spirits; traditional music and Celtic rock; and Brooklyn Bridge views.
Red Square (Map p182; ☎ 632-7407; www.mandalaybay.com; Mandalay Bay, 3950 Las Vegas Blvd S) A headless Lenin invites you behind the blood-red curtains for a tipple of vodka and caviar dished up on a solid ice bar.
rumjungle (Map p182; ☎ 632-7408; www.mandalaybay.com; Mandalay Bay, 3950 Las Vegas Blvd S) Dark, light or spicy rum flights from a pirate's towering selection of over 100 bottles – yarr, matey!
sidebar (Triple George Grill, p110) Imported cigarettes and cigars escort classic cocktails made with top-shelf spirits and an exquisitely robust wine list.

Catercorner from the Hard Rock, this $12-million beer hall and garden is a fawning replica of the original in Munich. Celebrate Oktoberfest all year with premium imported suds, big Bavarian pretzels, fair fräuleins, oom-pah-pah bands and trademark *gemütlichkeit* (congeniality).

⭐ HOOKAH LOUNGE Map pp190-1
☎ 731-6030; www.hookahlounge.com; 4147 S Maryland Parkway; admission free; 🕑 5pm-1am Sun-Thu, to 3am Fri & Sat; 🚌 109, 202
Next to Paymon's Mediterranean Café (p112), you can recline languorously with a water pipe stuffed with one of 20 premium flavored Egyptian tobaccos. Exotic fig-flavored cocktails are pricier than the off-Strip norm, but for ambience worthy of a pasha, why not?

⭐ NAPOLEON'S Map p182
☎ 946-7000; www.parislasvegas.com; Le Boulevard, Paris-Las Vegas, 3645 Las Vegas Blvd S; 🕑 4pm-2am; Ⓜ Bally's & Paris
Whisk yourself off to a never-neverland of 19th-century France, with overstuffed sofas and a luxurious menu of 100 types of bubbly, including vintage Dom Perignon – soar on a 'champagne flight.' The cigar humidor, dueling pianos and happy-hour carving station make it worth the stroll.

★ Rog'l
Alien at Star Trek: The Experience (p76)

Time spent on Earth Approximately 8¾ years and 6 days. **Biggest challenges for an alien living in Las Vegas** Making gold-pressed latinum (ie money) and keeping our wives at home. I've noticed that in Las Vegas, unlike on our planet, keeping females naked does not necessarily keep them at home. **Favorite casino game** When we got here, your fellow humans had the gambling all sewn up, so we had to send our Dabo table back through the time machine. **Favorite drink at Quark's Bar** Blood wine, which we water down for the humans and pass off as merlot. **In the Star Trek museum upstairs, don't miss** The mysterious-looking photon torpedo, in which Spock was buried in *Star Trek II: The Wrath of Khan*. **Strangest human to ever visit here** A little person dressed like a Klingon, who looked very fierce. I tried to do a little business with him, but he was already pretty far into his cups.

⭐ QUARK'S BAR Map pp190-1

☎ 888-462-6535; Deep Space Nine Promenade, Las Vegas Hilton, 3000 Paradise Rd; admission free; ⏰ 11:30am-10pm Sun-Thu, to 11pm Fri & Sat; Ⓜ Hilton

Ideal for seducing the alien of your dreams, this Star Trek–themed bar is a far-out, wacky place. Eavesdrop on sci-fi geeks debating the strategies of the Romulan Empire or the virtues of the Prime Directive as you get a knock-out punch from a 'Phaser Shot' or a dry ice–steaming 'Warp Core Breach' ($25).

⭐ TRIPLE 7 Map pp184-5

☎ 387-1896; www.mainstreetcasino .com; Main Street Station, 200 N Main St; admission free; ⏰ 24hr; 🚌 The Deuce

Sports fans and a crusty crowd of local gamblers flock to this gargantuan brewpub for Monday Night Football, happy hour and graveyard specials. The sushi and oyster bar, five microbrews on tap (look for specialty fruit beers) and cheap pub grub sate the punters.

⭐ SPAS

Some spas are reserved exclusively for hotel guests, including at the Bellagio, MGM Grand and Wynn. Day-use fees ($20 to $35) are normally waived for those receiving treatments ($100 to $200 per hour). Many spas have fitness

COOL POOLS

Vegas hotels are home to some truly spectacular aquatic hangouts, which are typically open during spring and summer. The coolest ones are the Garden of the Gods Oasis at Caesars Palace (p39); the Mandalay Bay (p48) wave pool and clothing-optional Moorea Beach Club; the MGM Grand (p40) 1000ft (300m) 'lazy river' ride; the lagoons and grottos at the Flamingo (p46); the gigantic 50-person party hot tub at TI (Treasure Island, p53); and the seductive Beach Club at the Hard Rock (p56), featuring swim-up blackjack, thatched cabañas with misting systems and legendary Rehab pool parties (non-guests $20 to $30) on summer Sunday afternoons.

facilities, so bring workout clothes and shoes.

BATHHOUSE Map p182

☎ 877-632-9636; www.thehotelatman dalaybay.com; THEhotel at Mandalay Bay, 3950 Las Vegas Blvd S; day pass $35; ⏰ 6am-8:30pm; 🚌 The Deuce

Designed for both sexes, this $25-million minimalist space defines hip. Organic skincare products include an 'aromapothecary' of massage oils blended to match your personality. Inside the spa are dramatic stone walls with waterfalls and chaise lounges by plunge pools.

SEE | SHOP | EAT | PLAY

PLAY

⭐ CANYON RANCH SPACLUB
Map p180

☎ 414-3600, 877-220-2688; www
.venetian.com; Grand Canal Shoppes,
Venetian, 3355 Las Vegas Blvd S; day pass
$35; 🕙 5:30am-10pm, café 7am-6pm;
🚌 Harrah's/Imperial Palace

Popular for side-by-side couples'
treatments, this health-minded
place offers over 100 activities –
from ayurvedic massage to rock
climbing – all priced à la carte. Day
passes include use of the high-
tech fitness facilities.

⭐ OASIS SPA Map p182

☎ 258-9308; www.luxor.com; Luxor,
3900 Las Vegas Blvd S; day pass $20;
🕙 24hr, closed 11:30pm Tue-6am Wed;
🚌 The Deuce

It's not quite pampering fit for
Queen Nefertiti, but this low-rollers'
place almost never closes. Day passes give you access to a crowded
dry sauna, steam bath, whirlpools,
Aveda aromatherapy showers and
the fitness center. Treatments are
bargain priced, but the real reason
to come is simply because you
can – at just about any hour.

⭐ PALMS SPA & AMP SALON
Map pp188-9

☎ 942-6937; www.palms.com; Palms,
4321 W Flamingo Rd; day pass $25;
🕙 6am-8pm; 🚌 202

Ultra-soft 'cashwear' robes, margarita and mojito skin cocktails,

and yoga by candelight – oh,
it's trendy to the max. So, what
are you waiting for? Relax by
the lushly landscaped lavender-
floored pool before enjoying a
couples' massage or an indulgent
'party prep' facial.

⭐ RED ROCK SPA

☎ 797-7878, 866-363-2872; www
.redrocklasvegas.com; Red Rock Casino
Resort Spa, 11011 W Charleston Blvd,
at I-215; day pass $35; 🕙 6am-8pm;
🚌 208

Far-flung west of the Strip, the
hottest spa in town emphasizes
holistic healing practices, from its
yoga gardens and lap pool to adventure spa offerings like guided
rock climbing in nearby Red Rock
Canyon (p146). Specialty mas-
sages include Thai-style or 'on the
rocks' with heated river stones.

⭐ ROCK SPA Map pp190-1

☎ 693-5554; www.hardrockhotel.com;
Hard Rock, 4455 Paradise Rd; day pass
$25; 🕙 6am-10pm; 🚌 108, 202

The glam factor here is super-
high. Inside the salon you'll find a
celebrity stylist who has tousled
the heads of David Bowie and Isa-
bella Rossellini. Among soothing
wood, rock and water elements,
the theme of the spa is 'recovery.'
Work off your most recent bender
with the latest fitness equipment,
maybe even by taking a boxing
class.

SPA BY MANDARA Map p182

☎ 946-4366; www.parislasvegas.com; Paris-Las Vegas, 3655 Las Vegas Blvd S; day pass $35; 🕑 6am-7pm; Ⓜ Bally's & Paris

With Matisse-styled tiling, this full-service European salon and spa evinces Balinese influences. Luxurious treatment rooms boast handcrafted tropical hardwood, artworks and silk carpets. The divine specialty of the house is facials.

⭐ LIVE MUSIC

Surf to www.yourlocalscene.com and www.sincitysounds.com for live-music listings and featured artists. Don't miss the crankin' indie-music fest Vegoose (see the boxed text, p127). Famed Austin-based alt-rock club **Emo's** (www.emos austin.com) is coming soon to downtown's Fremont St.

⭐ **BRENDAN'S IRISH PUB** Map pp188-9

☎ 365-7111; www.orleanscasino.com; Orleans, 4500 W Tropicana Ave; admission free; 🕑 shows 9pm; 🚌 free Strip shuttle

Blue-collar Brendan's in the Orleans casino stages rip-roarin' Zydeco Wednesday nights and Sunday-evening acoustic Celtic folk singalongs. It's nothing fancy, takes all comers and stocks Irish whiskeys, ales and more. For more authentic Irish pints, head to **McMullan's Irish Pub** (☎ 247 7000; 4650 W Tropicana Ave; 🕑 24hr) across the street.

⭐ **BUNKHOUSE SALOON** Map pp184-5

☎ 384-4536; www.bunkhouselv.com; 124 S 11th St; admission free; 🕑 24hr; 🚌 107

As you might have guessed, it's got a cowboy theme, with Old West art and saddles lying about. Gamewise, there are pool tables and darts, but the real draws are local DJs and live bands, anything from rockabilly to reggae, along with stand-up comedy and indie film nights. Wear your coolest vintage threads.

BEST CASINO LOUNGE ACTS

Casino lounges at New York-New York (p49), the Bellagio (p38) and the Mirage (p42) host free top-notch live bands. For vintage Vegas acts, cruise the North Strip hotels, especially the Sahara (p51), or casinos along downtown's Fremont St. The **Las Vegas Hilton** (Map pp190-1; ☎ 732-5111; www.lvhilton.com; 3000 Paradise Rd), where Elvis staged his Las Vegas comeback, carries on the tradition of big-name entertainers such as Wayne Newton and Tony Bennett in its cabaret showroom and theater.

SEE | SHOP | EAT | PLAY

PLAY

⭐ DOUBLE DOWN SALOON
Map pp190-1

☎ 791-5775; www.doubledownsaloon
.com; 4640 Paradise Rd; admission free;
🕑 24hr; 🚌 108

You just gotta love a punk bar where the tangy, blood-red house drink is named 'Ass Juice.' There's also a behavior code: 'You puke, you clean.' There's never a cover charge, and the low-roller drinks are cash only. Monday is the Bargain DJ Collective night, with lotsa lunatic-fringe bands other nights. Play pool, pinball, Asteroids or the legendary jukebox. To get here, enter off Swenson St.

⭐ HOUSE OF BLUES Map p182
☎ 632-7600; www.hob.com; Mandalay Bay, 3950 Las Vegas Blvd S; admission $15-100; 🕑 schedule varies; 🚌 The Deuce

Blues is the tip of the hog at this Mississippi Delta juke joint, where kickin' acts range from living legends to new rockers. Seating is limited, so show up early. Sight lines are good and the outsider folk-art decor is übercool.

⭐ THE JOINT Map pp190-1
☎ 693-5066; www.hardrockhotel.com; Hard Rock, 4455 Paradise Rd; admission $20-1000; 🕑 schedule varies; 🚌 108

Concerts at this intimate venue feel like private shows, even when David Bowie or the Killers are in town. It's a beacon for rock 'n' roll superstars. Most shows are standing-room only, with reservable VIP balcony seats upstairs.

House of Blues, Mandalay Bay

SEE | SHOP | EAT | PLAY

PLAY

LAS VEGAS CALENDAR

Las Vegas is a nonstop party 24/7/365, so it's almost superfluous to have more celebrations. But that doesn't stop anyone. Holidays (see p166) especially are taken to the max, with New Year's Eve along the Strip seeing the biggest crush of humanity this side of Times Sq. Major sports events also pack the city like a full house.

Contact the **Las Vegas Convention & Visitors Authority** (LVCVA; ☎ 877-847-4858; www.visitlasvegas.com) for a current calendar of events. The free alternative *Las Vegas Weekly* has up-to-the-minute events listings, as does the *Las Vegas Review-Journal*'s Friday 'Neon' entertainment guide.

May

Helldorado Days (www.lvhelldoradodays.com) Dating back to the 1930s, this historic hoedown features rodeo events, barbecues, country fiddlers and a recreation of an Old West frontier town by the Fremont Street Experience.

June, July & August

CineVegas (www.cinevegas.com) This prestigious nine-day film festival showcases indie flicks, first-time directors and some major Hollywood names like Nicolas Cage and Dennis Hopper, who chairs its creative board.

World Series of Poker (www.worldseriesofpoker.com) High stakes gamblers, casino employees and celebrities match wits in over 40 tournaments running from late June to early August. Free public viewing is encouraged.

October

Vegoose (www.vegoose.com) Coinciding with Halloween, this upstart music and arts festival is notorious for live indie bands, interactive performance art and a full weekend of costumed partying.

November

Aviation Nation (www.aviationnation.org) At Nellis Air Force Base, this is the nation's most famous military and civilian air show. The Thunderbirds, an aerial demonstration team, usually zooms in on the last day.

December

Wrangler National Finals Rodeo (www.nfrexperience.com) This hugely popular 10-day event features professional rodeo cowboys competing in a half-dozen adrenaline-driven events, including steer wrestling and bull riding.

⭐ MATTEO'S UNDERGROUND LOUNGE
☎ 293-0098; www.matteodining.com; 1305 Arizona St, Boulder City; admission $5-10; ☽ shows usually Wed-Sun
A helluva drive from the Strip, this locals-only hangout near Hoover Dam (p144) is paradise for indie-music lovers. Some of Sin City's best rock and jazz bands play underground (literally) shows here. Call first to check schedules.

⭐ SAND DOLLAR BLUES LOUNGE Map pp188-9
☎ 871-6651; 3355 Spring Mountain Rd; admission Tue-Sat $5; ☽ 24hr; 🚌 203
When you're on your last dime, drive to this dive. A few doors down from a Harley repair shop, this unpretentious club is the only one in town featuring live jazz and blues nightly after 10pm. It's smoky, casual and has a nautical theme, video poker and pool tables. It draws a tough local crowd. To get here, enter off Polaris Ave.

⭐ ULTRA LOUNGES & AFTER HOURS
The strip club Seamless (p136) transforms nightly into a sensual after-hours party spot. Look for the newly opened Playboy Club inside the Palms (p58).

⭐ DRAI'S Map p182
☎ 737-0555; Barbary Coast, 3595 Las Vegas Blvd S; admission $20-30;

☽ midnight-dawn Wed-Sun; 🚌 Flamingo/Caesars Palace
Ready for a scene straight outta Hollywood? Drai is an LA producer and restaurateur to the starlets. Things don't really get going until 3am, when DJs spinning progressive discs keep the fashion plates from being too bitchy.

⭐ FORTY DEUCE Map p182
☎ 632-9442; www.fortydeuce.com; lower level, Mandalay Place, 3930 Las Vegas Blvd S; admission $10-25; ☽ 10:30pm-late Thu-Mon; 🚌 The Deuce
A speakeasy vibe pervades this sexy, but petite bi-level club. Ignore the crazy bachelorette antics and feast your eyes instead on the smoking-hot traditional burlesque acts backed up by a brassy three-piece jazz band. Acts appear on stage every 90 minutes, starting before midnight.

⭐ GHOSTBAR Map pp188-9
☎ 942-7777; http://las-vegas.n9ne group.com; Palms, 4321 W Flamingo Rd; admission $10-25; ☽ 8pm-late; 🚌 202
With its 360-degree panoramas and sci-fi decor, the Palms' 55th-floor watering hole pulls in a clubby crowd that's frequently thick with celebs, from hip-hop stars to sports stars. The line-up of hoochie mamas and wannabe gangstas can be tiresome, but the views are to die for. Dress to kill.

⭐ MIX Map p182
☎ 632-9500; www.chinagrillmgt.com/mixlv; 64th fl, THEhotel at Mandalay Bay, 3950 Las Vegas Blvd S; admission after 10pm $20-25; ⏰ 5pm-2am Sun-Tue, to 4am Wed, Fri & Sat; 🚌 The Deuce
Arrive before sunset and take a free glass elevator ride up to this sky-high restaurant lounge with one of the most breathtaking views in Vegas – and that's even before glimpsing the wall-to-wall leather seating and the champagne bar. Go hobnobbing with the glitterati on the vertiginous open-air patio.

⭐ PUSSYCAT DOLLS LOUNGE Map p182
☎ 731-7873; www.pcdlounge.com; Caesars Palace, 3570 Las Vegas Blvd S; admission $20-30; ⏰ 10pm-late Tue-Sat; Ⓜ Flamingo/Caesars Palace
Lingerie-clad ladies do a little aerial swinging, play rub-a-dub dub in a tub and flaunt sexy song-and-dance numbers. Busta Rhymes got so excited that he jumped on stage during the club's grand opening. Look for celebs such as Eva Longoria of *Desperate Housewives* making surprise appearances at this SoCal import.

⭐ ROMANCE AT TOP OF THE WORLD Map p180
☎ 380-7711; www.stratospherehotel.com; 107th fl, Stratosphere, 2000 Las Vegas Blvd S; elevator ride $10; ⏰ 4pm-late; 🚌 The Deuce
There's just no place to get any higher in Vegas without the approval of an air-traffic controller. From Wednesday to Saturday evenings, smooth jazz accompanies the 'elevated' martinis swilled by a moneyed crowd of cocktail-hour couples.

⭐ TABÚ Map p182
☎ 891-7183; www.mgmgrand.com; MGM Grand, 3799 Las Vegas Blvd S; admission $15; ⏰ 10pm-late Tue-Sun; Ⓜ MGM Grand
MGM's groundbreaking ultra lounge is all sensual sophistication. DJs spin Euro house music to an interactive backdrop while stunning hostesses who also happen to be models mix cocktails tableside.

TOP FIVE DRINKS WITH VIP VIEWS
> Fontana Bar (Bellagio, p38) – privileged views of the Bellagio's dancing fountains and live jazz
> Foundation Room (p131) – the VIPs who lounge here definitely don't need this book!
> ghostbar (opposite) – a pimped-out panorama at the top of the Palms
> Mix (left) – sky-high cocktails and a fairytale glass elevator ride
> Romance at Top of the World (left) – soar above the Strip, thanks to masterful martinis

V

SEE | SHOP | EAT | PLAY

PLAY

⭐ **TANGERINE** Map p180
☎ 894-7580; www.tangerineclub.com; TI (Treasure Island), 3300 Las Vegas Blvd S; admission $10-20; ⏰ 6pm-4am Tue-Sat; 🚌 The Deuce

TI turns up the heat with its orange-flavored ultra lounge featuring a showy open-air Stripside patio. DJs spin pop, house and hip-hop, while burlesque dancers shimmy on the bartop hourly, starting around 9pm.

⭐ **V BAR** Map p182
☎ 414-3200; www.venetian.com; Venetian, 3355 Las Vegas Blvd S; admission free; ⏰ 5pm-4am; Ⓜ Harrah's/Imperial Palace

Starlets, agents and young fashionistas air-kiss inside this glam minimalist lounge. The acid jazz and low-key house music are mere accoutrements, since the low lighting, secluded sitting areas and sturdy martinis encourage intimate behavior among the very best of strangers. Service can be iffy.

⭐ **NIGHTCLUBS**

The Strip's megaresorts are on par with LA and NYC in the arena of wildly extravagant hangouts. Ladies sometimes get in free before midnight, especially on weeknights. Surf to www.clubplanet.com and www.vegas.com for sneak peeks, events calendars and VIP passes.

⭐ **BODY ENGLISH** Map pp190-1
☎ 693-4000; www.hardrockhotel.com; Hard Rock, 4455 Paradise Rd; admission $20-30; ⏰ 10:30pm-4am Fri-Sun; 🚌 108, 202

Tangerine, TI (Treasure Island)

The Hard Rock's posh club offers VIP pampering. Booth reservations require one bottle ($300 minimum) per foursome, but there's also a big bar for the hoi polloi. The dress code is denim to diamonds and the bumpin' tunes are rock, hip-hop and house.

⭐ EMPIRE BALLROOM Map p182
☎ 737-7376; www.empireballroom .com; 3765 Las Vegas Blvd S; admission $10-20; 🕒 10pm-6am Thu-Sun; Ⓜ MGM Grand; Ⓟ valet $5

The pumping sound system at this Stripside club channels pure rock 'n' roll driven by local and touring rock bands. After hours, it morphs into a comfy sofa spot with up-tempo DJs and a supersized dance floor overhung by a fantastical chandelier.

⭐ FOUNDATION ROOM
Map p182
☎ 391-9979; www.hob.com; 43rd fl, Mandalay Bay, 3950 Las Vegas Blvd S; admission $30; 🕒 by invitation only; 🚌 The Deuce

House of Blues' (p126) exclusive club atop M-Bay hosts after-show parties in a luxurious lounge with exotic decor. Celebs like Andre Agassi hold court, while DJs and special events enliven the vibe. Call or email to get on the guest list for public events, like Monday's **Godspeed** (www.godspeedlv.com).

⭐ ICE Map p182
☎ 699-9888; www.icelasvegas.com; 200 E Harmon Ave; admission $5-20; 🕒 10pm-4am Tue & Fri-Sun; 🚌 105; Ⓟ valet $5

It's no contest: Vegas' most stellar DJs spin at this off-Strip jewel box. Deep house, trance and techno play in the main multistoried dance hall, while the sidecar lounge heaves with hip-hop, retro '80s and mash-ups. Shortish lines outside the door ease you in to see the honeys lickety-split.

⭐ JET Map p180
☎ 792-7900; www.lightgroup.com; Mirage, 3400 Las Vegas Blvd S; admission $20-30; 🕒 10:30pm-4am Fri, Sat & Mon; 🚌 The Deuce

A sophisticated tri-environment club, Jet has broken the sound barrier in racing to the creamy top of Vegas' nightlife. Follow the flickering candles and tiny staircase made for strutting onto the mainstream dance floor, or sidle into more intimate lounges where the beats run to deep house and hip-hop.

⭐ LIGHT Map p182
☎ 693-8300; www.lightlv.com; Bellagio, 3600 Las Vegas Blvd S; admission $30; 🕒 10:30pm-4am Thu-Sun; Ⓜ Bally's & Paris

Draped with velvet, boxy Light encourages socializing in plush surrounds while professional hosts push top-shelf bottle service. Mainstream dance sounds predominate. If you want to chill, book a VIP booth. Since it's a celeb hangout (think Leo and his entourage), reservations are recommended.

⭐ OPM Map p182

☎ 387-3840; www.o-pmlv.com; Forum Shops, 3500 Las Vegas Blvd S; admission $20-30; ☽ 10pm-dawn Wed-Sun; Ⓜ Flamingo/Caesars Palace

The throbbing beats at this faux-Asian hideaway may peak earlier than at other places, but there's rarely a long line. At the moment, Latin rules Wednesday with hip-hop straight through the weekend, including hyphy on Sunday night. Bites from downstairs Chinois (p94) are served. Strict dress code.

⭐ PURE Map p182

☎ 731-7873; www.purethenightclub .com; Caesars Palace, 3570 Las Vegas Blvd S; admission $10-30; ☽ 10pm-late Fri-Tue; Ⓜ Flamingo/Caesars Palace

With gorgeous female DJs much of the time, this chic modern space is all done up in hues of electric blue, white and silver. Crowds of fine young thangs lounge inside a labyrinth of rooms that feel a lot like LA, all leading up to a gorgeous Strip-view patio. Strict dress code.

⭐ RAIN Map pp188-9

☎ 942-6832; http://las-vegasn9negroup .com; Palms, 4321 W Flamingo Rd; admission $10-25; ☽ 11pm-5am Thu, 10pm-5am Fri & Sat; 🚌 202

Britney Spears once threw an impromptu concert while partying at this club, which is immersed in color and motion. The bamboo dance floor appears to float on a layer of fountains. Fog and pyrotechnics set the sybaritic mood, as seen on MTV's *Real World*. Warning: the Palms' new Moon nightclub inside the Playboy Tower may upstage this scene soon.

⭐ TAO Map p180

☎ 388-8588; www.taolasvegas.com; Venetian, 3355 Las Vegas Blvd S; admission $20-30; ☽ 10pm-5am Thu-Sat; Ⓜ Harrah's/Imperial Palace

Modeled after the Asian-themed NYC nightclub, here svelte go-go girls covered only by strategically placed flowers splash in bathtubs while another in yogi garb assumes the lotus position on a

---

THE BIG NIGHT BEFORE THE MORNING AFTER

Looking to organize one last wild night out for your fave bachelor or bachelorette? Besides Vegas' strip clubs (p134) and Forty Deuce (p128), the Palms (p58) and Hard Rock (p56) casino hotels cater to the on-the-verge crowd.

pedestal high above the risqué dance floor, where Paris Hilton lookalikes forego enlightenment to bump-and-grind to earthy hip-hop instead.

⭐ GAY & LESBIAN LAS VEGAS

East of the Strip alongside the UNLV campus, the Fruit Loop triangle is an island of flamboy-ance in a sea of straightness. Pick up a free copy of *QVegas* (www .qvegas.com) magazine at **Get Booked** (☎ 737-7780; 4640 S Paradise Rd; ⏲ 10am-midnight Sun-Thu, 10am-2am Fri & Sat), a lesbigay retailer. Also surf to www.outlasvegas.com and www.gayvegas.com.

⭐ BUFFALO Map pp190-1

☎ 733 8355; 4640 Paradise Rd; admis sion free; ⏲ 24hr; 🚌 108

Cruisy Levis-and-leather-clad boyz hang at this bar, which has pool tables, Friday-night and Sunday-afternoon beer busts and plenty of tough-looking but friendly fellows letting the good times roll.

⭐ CHARLIE'S Map p182

☎ 876-1844; www.charlieslasvegas .com; 5012 S Arville St; admission free; ⏲ 7pm-late Thu-Mon; 🚌 201

Don't cry for me, Brokeback Mountain. Vegas has its own country-and-western bar for gay men. It's rowdiest on weekends when there are beer and liquor busts and also during post-rodeo 'survivor' parties. Show up early for two-step and line-dance lessons some nights.

⭐ FREE ZONE Map pp190-1

☎ 794-2300; www.freezonelv.com; 610 E Naples Dr; admission free; ⏲ 24hr; 🚌 108

Every night is a party at this hang-out. Sunday and Monday are for free pool and karaoke, Tuesday is ladies night, Thursday is boyz night and Friday and Saturday nights feature the Queens of Las Vegas drag cabaret.

⭐ GIPSY Map pp190-1

☎ 731-1919; www.gipsylv.net; 4605 S Paradise Rd; admission $5-10; ⏲ 9pm-late; 🚌 108

It was once the premier gay dance club in town, and there's always a mixed crowd at this giant thumpa-thumpa nightclub a stone's throw south of the Hard Rock. Look for Illusions Cabaret drag shows on Sunday night and Latin grooves on Monday.

⭐ GOODTIMES Map pp190-1

☎ 736-9494; www.goodtimeslv.com; 1775 E Tropicana Ave; admission free; ⏲ 24hr; 🚌 201

A men's club where conversation rules, but there's also a steel dance floor, video poker, pool tables and a legendary Monday liquor bust from 11pm to 4am. It's built next door to the Liberace Museum (p75). A coincidence? We think not.

⭐ KRÄVE Map p182

☎ 836-0830; www.kravelasvegas.com; 3663 Las Vegas Blvd S; admission $5-20; 🕐 10pm-3am Sun-Thu, 11pm-3am Fri & Sat; 🚌 The Deuce

The Strip's only gay club is a glam place packed wall-to-wall with hard bodies, plush booth seating and VIP cabañas, and even 'airotic' flyboys. The side lounge has karaoke, salsa and girls-only nights. Keep an eye open for weekend after-hours events. Enter off Harmon Ave outside Desert Passage.

⭐ LA CAGE Map p180

☎ 794-9433, 877-892-7469; www.riviera hotel.com; Riviera, 2901 Las Vegas Blvd S; admission $55; 🕐 7:30pm Wed-Mon; 🚌 The Deuce

In this female-impersonator revue, the award-winning Frank Marino (who cameoed in *Miss Congeniality 2*) acts as a catty Joan Rivers, dispensing naughty jokes and remarks between mostly lip-synched impersonations of Diana Ross, Cher and Liza Minnelli.

⭐ PIRANHA Map pp190-1

☎ 791-0100; www.gipsylv.net; 4633 Paradise Rd; admission $5-20; 🕐 9pm-late; 🚌 108

Sin City's newest gay nightclub is also its sexiest, featuring fireplace patios, aquariums and waterfalls, plus the luxurious 8½ ultra lounge. A rainbow variety of dance club events includes DJ-driven Milk Mondays (the slogan: 'HOMO-genizing Las Vegas'), hip-hop Bling Tuesdays and ladies-only Orchid Wednesdays. There's often no cover before 11pm.

⭐ SUEDE Map pp190-1

☎ 791-3463; www.gipsylv.net; 4640 Paradise Rd; 🕐 5pm-late Wed-Sun; 🚌 108

In the heart of the Fruit Loop, this oh-so-casual restaurant and lounge is the spot for drag and female-impersonator cabaret acts on weekends, with fabulous gay karaoke earlier in the week.

⭐ TOUCAN'S BAR & GRILLE Map pp190-1

☎ 735-4400; www.toucanslv.com; 4503 Paradise Rd; 🕐 11am-1am; 🚌 108, 202

Find fuel in the Fruit Loop at this welcoming queer restaurant. Take refuge at the pool tables, or show up for riotous lip-sync contests and trivia, pajama karaoke, TV and bingo nights.

⭐ STRIP CLUBS

Vegas is the original adult Disney-land. Prostitution may be illegal, but there are plenty of places offering the illusion of sex on demand. Unescorted women are welcome at some clubs, but not on busy nights. Bring cash for tips.

⭐ CLUB PARADISE Map pp190-1
☎ 734-7990; www.clubparadise .net; 4416 Paradise Rd; admission $20; 🕑 5pm-6am; 🚌 108
Choreographed showgirls perform here, with specialty acts thrown into the bizarre mix. You might see former Cirque du Soleil acrobats or women in eveningwear straight out of a Miss USA pageant. Strip teases are tame, but they've got showbiz appeal.

⭐ GIRLS OF GLITTER GULCH Map pp184-5
☎ 385-4774; www.glittergulchlv.com; 20 E Fremont St; admission free, 2-drink minimum; 🕑 24hr; 🚌 The Deuce
As you experience Fremont St (p71), you can't help but notice this topless joint that downtown boosters wish would just go away. Inside you'll find surprisingly friendly dancers and a crowd of Middle American tourists.

⭐ OLYMPIC GARDEN Map pp186-7
☎ 385-9361; www.ogvegas.com; 1531 Las Vegas Blvd S; admission $20; 🕑 24hr; 🚌 The Deuce
The unpretentious OG wins high marks from topless-club aficionados – and the nickname 'Silicone

Valley' from the competition. Up to 50 dancers work at any given time, thus there's something to please everyone. Studs strip for the ladies upstairs Wednesday through Sunday.

⭐ SAPPHIRE Map pp188-9
☎ 796-6000; www.sapphirelasvegas .com; 3025 S Industrial Rd; admission $25-30; 🕑 24hr; 🚌 105
Billed as the 'world's largest adult entertainment complex,' with a stable of thousands of entertainers and VIP skyboxes overlooking the showroom cheesily dominated

---

GIRLS JUST WANNA HAVE FUN

The dancers at Rio's **Chippendales Theater** (Map pp100-9; ☎ 777-7776, www.playrio.com; admission $35-75) seem more concerned with basking in the spotlight than giving the girls a feel. Private sky boxes, a spacious cocktail lounge and plush bathroom with a 'gossip pit' are the icing on the hunky cake. But you can touch the lovely lads of Excalibur's **Thunder Down Under** (Map p182; ☎ 597-7600; www.excalibur.com; admission $40-50), who provide nonstop fun and flirting...a bachelorette-party must! The down-and-dirty Men of Olympus strut their stuff upstairs at the Olympic Garden (left), while the Men of Sapphire fire up the weekends-only Playgirl Club at Sapphire (above).

by a story-high martini glass. Beefy men strip upstairs in the Playgirl Club on Friday and Saturday nights.

SEAMLESS Map pp188-9
☎ 227-5200; www.seamlessclub.com; 4740 S Arville St; admission $20-30; 24hr; 🚌 201

Erasing the thin line between strip clubs and nightclubs, this high-concept spot switches gears 'seamlessly' at 4am every night, with an after-hours dance party that goes till 11am. Expect designer furnishings, drop-dead gorgeous dancers sauntering along a glass catwalk and VIP service all the way, starting with an exhibitionists' parking garage.

⭐ PRODUCTION SHOWS

Leaving Las Vegas without seeing a show must be a crime. The most in-demand tix are for Cirque du Soleil extravaganzas and straight-off-Broadway musicals. Old-school shows involve minimal plot with a variety of kitschy song, dance and magic numbers. A grab-bag of erotically themed shows, from rock musicals to late-night vampire revues, aren't really worth the money.

⭐ BEACHER'S MADHOUSE
Map pp190-1
☎ 699-7844; www.beachersmadhouse .com; Hard Rock, 4455 Paradise Rd; admission $25; call for schedules

A-list celebs in the VIP box may steal your attention away from this interactive comedy show, where spectators get pulled up on stage to sing their hearts out like the next *American Idol*. Expect frenetic frat-boy antics, sick stand-up and a little magic in this bawdy, short-attention-span theater.

⭐ FASHIONISTAS Map p182
☎ 836-0833; www.fashionistastheshow .com; Krāve Theater, 3663 Las Vegas Blvd S; admission $55-88; 9:30pm Tue-Sat; 🚌 The Deuce

An imaginative erotic show with an edgy soundtrack, its inventive choreography prettifies a story based on none other than a porn movie directed by John Stagliano. The flamboyant costumes by themselves are unforgettable, let alone the simulated S&M scenes. Enter off Harmon Ave.

BEHIND THE SCENES

Bally's (Map p182; ☎ 946-4567, 877-374-7469) runs one-hour backstage tours of its long-running spectacular, Donn Arden's *Jubilee* (opposite). The tours ($15, with show-ticket purchase $10) offer a sneak peek inside the hidden lives of showgirls and chorus boys, starting at 11am Monday, Wednesday and Saturday.

⭐ FOLIES BERGÈRE Map p182

☎ 800-829-9034; www.tropicanalv .com; Tropicana, 3801 Las Vegas Blvd S; admission $50-60; 🕑 7:30pm (covered) & 10pm (topless) Mon, Wed, Thu & Sat, 8:30pm (topless) Tue & Fri

A gaudy tribute to the Parisian Music Hall, Vegas' longest-running production still has some of the most beautiful showgirls in town. Sticking to a formulaic Francophile theme, over-the-top song-and-dance numbers include the inevitable can-can routine, plus a comedic juggler to lighten it up.

⭐ JUBILEE! Map p182

☎ 800-237-7469; www.harrahs.com; Bally's, 3645 Las Vegas Blvd S; admission $65-82; 🕑 7:30pm & 10:30pm; Ⓜ Bal-ly's & Paris

Girls, girls, girls! It's a showgirl production that Vegas wouldn't be Vegas without. As it started, so does it end: with lots of knockers, twinkling rhinestones and enormous headdresses on display. If you can forgive the giant helping of cheese, it's a riot.

⭐ KÀ Map p182

☎ 877-264-1844; http://ka.com; MGM Grand, 3799 Las Vegas Blvd S; admission $69-150; 🕑 6:30pm & 9:30pm Tue-Sat; Ⓜ MGM Grand

So what's the hook that's made it the hottest ticket in town? Instead of a stage, there's a grid of moving

platforms for a frenzy of martial arts inspired performances. Weak storytelling mars the sensuous tale of imperial twins, mysterious destinies, love and conflict. Premium seats hold court at the back.

⭐ LA FEMME Map p182

☎ 800-929-1111; www.mgmgrand .com; MGM Grand, 3799 Las Vegas Blvd S; admission $59; 🕑 8pm & 10:30pm Wed-Mon; Ⓜ MGM Grand

Za, za, zoom. The classiest topless show in town defines sexy. The 100% red room's intimate bordello feel oozes amour. Onstage, balletic dancers straight from Paris' Crazy Horse Saloon perform provocative cabaret numbers interspersed with voyeuristic *l'art du nu* vignettes. *Zut alors* – It's a classy peep show par excellence.

⭐ LEGENDS IN CONCERT
Map p180

☎ 877-777-7664; www.imperialpalace .com; Imperial Palace, 3535 Las Vegas Blvd S; admission incl 1 drink $35-60; 🕑 7:30pm & 10pm Mon-Sat; Ⓜ Harrah's/Imperial Palace; ♿

It's been around since the early '80s. Vegas' top pop-star impersonator show features real talent – no lip-synching allowed. Video screens beside the stage show real-life concert clips of the performers, while the back-up dancers boogie up a *Saturday Night Fever* storm.

⭐ LOVE Map p180

☎ 792-7777, 800-963-9634; www.cir quedusoleil.com; Mirage, 3400 Las Vegas Blvd S; admission $69-150; ⏰ 7:30pm & 10:30pm Thu-Mon; 🚌 The Deuce; ♿
Vegas' newest and most bizarre Cirque du Soleil hit began as an idea of the late George Harrison. Using the Abbey Road master tapes, it psychedelically fuses the musical legacy of the Beatles with high-energy dance (but none of the troupe's signature acrobatics) as it trips through the Fab Four's story.

⭐ MYSTÈRE Map p180

☎ 796-9999, 800-392-1999; www .cirquedusoleil.com; TI (Treasure Island), 3300 Las Vegas Blvd S; admission $60-95; ⏰ 7:30pm & 10:30pm Wed-Sat, 4:30pm & 7:30pm Sun; 🚌 The Deuce; ♿
Cirque du Soleil director Franco Dragone does for theater what Dali did for painting. His evocative celebration of life begins with a pair of babies making their way in a world filled with strange creatures. A misguided clown's humorous antics are interspersed with agile feats of acrobats, aerialists and dancers. It's still the cheapest Cirque ticket in town.

⭐ O Map p182

☎ 796-9999, 800-963-9634; www.cirque dusoleil.com; Bellagio, 3600 Las Vegas Blvd S; admission $94-150; ⏰ 7:30pm & 10:30pm Wed-Sun; Ⓜ Bally's & Paris

Lance Burton: Master Magician theater, Monte Carlo

LAS VEGAS IDOL

Ellis Island Casino (Map pp190-1; ☎ 733-8901; 4178 Koval Lane) An Old Vegas lounge with red highbacked booths; tasty microbrews and nightly karaoke are a big hit with local hipsters.
Harrah's Piano Bar (near Carnaval Court, p120) It's TJ's All-Star Karaoke Party on Friday and Saturday nights, with plasma screens, impressionists and stand-up comedy acts interspersed with amateur lounge lizards.
House of Blues (p126) 'Rock Star Karaoke' is the place to be on Monday and Tuesday nights. Hop on stage with the live band (they sing back-up) and everyone's your groupie.

'Eau' (French for water) is Cirque du Soleil's original epic venture into aquatic theater. A talented international cast – performing in, on and above the precious liquid – surveys drama through the ages. Though it's a spectacular feat of imagination and engineering, this one-tricky pony often disappoints.

⭐ COMEDY & MAGIC

Big-name comedians often headline at the MGM Grand (p40), Hilton (see the boxed text, p125), Flamingo (p46), Golden Nugget (p56) and House of Blues (p126).

⭐ **COMEDY STOP** Map p182
☎ 734-2714; www.comedystop.com; Tropicana, 3801 Las Vegas Blvd S;

admission incl 1 drink $20; ⏰ 8pm (nonsmoking) & 10:30pm (smoking); Ⓜ MGM Grand
Be sure to check out the A-list funny men and women cracking up the crowd at the Trop. You can find them in the mezzanine-level cabaret at this Atlantic City export.

⭐ **THE IMPROV** Map p180
☎ 800-838-9383; www.harrahs.com; Harrah's, 3475 Las Vegas Blvd S; admission $27.50; ⏰ 8:30pm & 10:30pm Tue-Sun; Ⓜ Harrah's/Imperial Palace
The Vegas franchise of this New York–based chain has that signature Big Apple brick backdrop. The spotlight is firmly cast on many of the touring stand-up headliners of the moment, often polished by recent late-night TV appearances.

⭐ **LANCE BURTON: MASTER MAGICIAN** Map p182
☎ 730-7160, 877-386-8224; www.lance burton.com; Monte Carlo, 3770 Las Vegas Blvd S; admission $67-73; ⏰ 7pm Tue-Sat, 10pm Tue & Sat; Ⓜ MGM Grand;
There are lots of magicians in Vegas, but few as engaging or talented as Lance Burton. Grand illusions include a signature 'flying' white Corvette, but Lance differs from the rest of the pack by emphasizing sleight-of-hand tricks and other close-up magic. The 1275-seat theater built for the master doesn't contain a bad seat.

Luxor casino hotel, containing an IMAX theater

⭐ PENN & TELLER Map pp188-9

☎ 777-7776; www.pennandteller.com; Rio, 3700 W Flamingo Rd; admission $60-75; 🕙 9pm Wed-Mon; 🚌 free Strip shuttle

This intellectual odd couple (one talks, the other doesn't) has been creating illusions for over two decades, spellbinding the audience with wit, charm and some amazing stunts such as catching bullets in their teeth. The gimmick is they actually explain some (but not all) of their tricks to the audience.

⭐ SECOND CITY Map p182

☎ 733-3333; www.secondcity.com; Flamingo, 3555 Las Vegas Blvd S; admission $40; 🕙 8pm Thu-Tue & 10:30pm Thu-Sat; Ⓜ Flamingo/Caesars Palace

The most reliable, best-value sketch comedy acts are scripted by this national chain of comedy theaters. An ambitious 75 minutes of hilarity including brilliant flashes of improv are staged inside the Flamingo's showroom.

⭐ WORLD'S GREATEST MAGIC SHOW Map p180

☎ 952-8000, 800-633-1777; www.greek islesvegas.com; Greek Isles, 305 Convention Center Dr; admission $65-75; 🕙 6pm Sat-Thu, 8:15pm Fri; Ⓜ Convention Center; ♿

Two big advantages here: you're not stuck with one performer for the whole 90-minute show, and it's family friendly. Expect a fast-paced merry-go-round of up to a dozen different magicians at this low-roller casino.

 CINEMAS

Check **Fandango** (☎ 800-326-3264; www.fandango.com) for showtimes and ticketing. The Bunkhouse Saloon (p125) screens independent films most Sunday nights.

⭐ **BRENDEN PALMS CASINO**
Map pp188-9
☎ 507-4849; www.brendentheatres.com; Palms, 4321 W Flamingo Rd; admission $6-10; 🚌 202; ♿
Home to the CineVegas film festival (see the boxed text, p127), the swankest off-Strip movieplex is fitted with IMAX and Lucasfilm

THX digital sound, plus stadium seating for superior sightlines.

⭐ **LAS VEGAS DRIVE-IN**
☎ 646-3565 4150; W Carey Ave, east of N Rancho Dr; admission $4-6; 🕐 gates open at 6:30pm; ♿
One of the only drive-ins in the entire state of Nevada, this old-fashioned place screens up to six double features daily. Bring your buddies, grab a bucket of popcorn and put your feet up on the dashboard.

⭐ **LUXOR IMAX THEATRE**
Map p182
☎ 262-4555; Luxor, 3900 Las Vegas Blvd S; admission $12; 🕐 hourly 9am-11pm; 🚌 The Deuce; ♿
Luxor's theater projects onto a seven-story, wall-mounted (rather

---

SPORTS & CONCERT MEGA-VENUES

Las Vegas Motor Speedway (☎ 644-4444, 800-644-4444; www.lvms.com; 7000 Las Vegas Blvd N) Nascar, Indy racing, drag racing and racecar ride-alongs (p70).

Mandalay Bay Events Center (Map p182; ☎ 877-632-7800; www.mandalaybay.com; 3950 Las Vegas Blvd S) Boxing, headliner concerts and bull riding.

MGM Grand Garden Arena (Map p182; ☎ 891-8777, 877-880-0880; www.mgmgrand .com; 3799 Las Vegas Blvd S) Boxing, superstar concerts and tennis.

Orleans Arena (Map pp188-9; ☎ 284-7777, 888-234-2334; www.orleansarena.com; Orleans, 4500 W Tropicana Ave) Arena football, boxing, hockey, motorsports and concerts.

Sam Boyd Stadium (☎ 739-3267, 866-388-3267; www.samboydstadium.com; 7000 E Russell Rd) UNLV college football, motorsports and concerts.

Thomas & Mack Center (Map pp190-1; ☎ 739-3267, 866-388-3267; www.thomasandmack .com; UNLV campus, 4505 S Maryland Parkway) College basketball, concerts, motorsports and rodeo.

PLAY

than curved overhead) screen, but the images are 10 times more detailed than conventional cinemas, not to mention the 15,000-watt digital surround-sound system.

⭐ REGAL VILLAGE SQUARE

☎ 221-2283; 9400 W Sahara Ave; admission $6-10; 🚌 204; ♿

Las Vegas doesn't have any art-house cinemas, but this multiplex way the hell out west of the Strip usually has at least a couple of independent flicks up on the marquee.

⭐ SPORTS

Although Vegas doesn't have any professional sports franchises, it's a very sports-savvy town. There are a half-dozen all-sports radio stations and you can wager on just about anything at casino race and sports books (p32). Nearly every watering hole in town runs Monday-night football specials. Some of the most lively parties happen at Triple 7 brewpub (p123) and the Hard Rock (p56).

World-class championship boxing draws fans from all around the globe. **UNLV Runnin' Rebels** (☎ 739-3267, 866-388-3267; http://unlv.rivals.com) college football and basketball teams enjoy a patriotic local following. The minor-league **Las Vegas 51s** (☎ 386-7200; www.lv51.com; Cashman Field, 850 Las Vegas Blvd N) baseball team (as in alien-infested Area 51 in southern Nevada), a franchise of the MLB Los Angeles Dodgers, plays home games from April to August. Feeding the NHL Calgary Flames, the minor-league **Las Vegas Wranglers** (☎ 471-7825; www.lasvegaswranglers.com) ice-hockey team faces off October to April. From January to May, the **Las Vegas Gladiators** (☎ 731-4977; www.lvgladiators.com) plays arena football, which is faster, leaner and more aggressive than regular NFL American-style football. Auto racing at the Las Vegas Motor Speedway is enormously popular. The premier rodeo event of the year is the Wranglers National Finals Rodeo (p127).

Ticketmaster (☎ 474-4000; www.ticketmaster.com) sells tickets for some major sporting events.

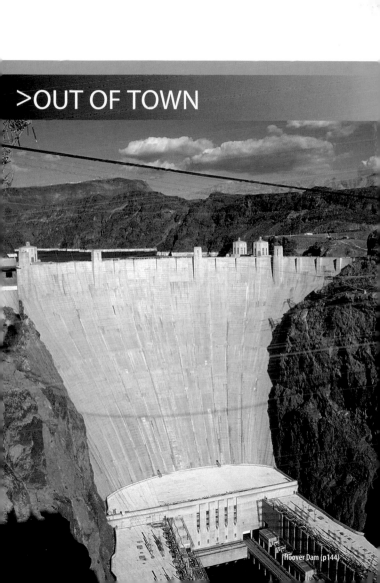

>OUT OF TOWN

Hoover Dam (p144)

HOOVER DAM TO THE VALLEY OF FIRE

The art-deco **Hoover Dam** (726ft; 221m) is a striking beauty, with its graceful concrete curve filling a dramatic canyon, backed by brilliant blue waters. The dam was built primarily to control floods on the lower Colorado River, which irrigates a million acres of land in the USA and half a million in Mexico.

When you tire of admiring the view and pretending to jump the railing, make a beeline for the refrigerated gift shop to pick up unique, all-American novelties for your loved ones: 'Dam Proud to be an American' bumper stickers; super-coolio mesh hats; Hoover Dam–shaped ceramic mugs – you name it, bub.

If you're driving, ditch your vehicle in the parking lot before you reach the dam. Bus trips from Vegas are a good deal and guarantee a ticket for the tour, during which you'll ride an elevator 50 stories down to view the massive power generators, then zoom back up to gawk at the 30ft (9m) Winged Figures of the Republic.

Backtracking a few miles, the scenic drive around **Lake Mead National Recreation Area** (☎ 702-293-8906/8990; www.nps.gov/lame; admission $5; ☻ 24hr) follows Northshore Rd, passing hiking trails, beaches, marinas and birding spots, up to Overton's **Lost City Museum** (☎ 702-397-2193; http://dmla.clan .lib.nv.us/docs/museums/lost/lostcity.htm; 721 S Moapa Valley Blvd; adult/child/student & senior $3/free/2; ☻ 8:30am-4:30pm) of Native American culture. It's past the turn-off to **Valley of Fire State Park** (☎ 702-397-2088; http://parks.nv.gov/vf.htm; admission $6; ☻ 24hr), a masterpiece of desert scenery. This fantasyland of wondrous shapes was carved by wind and water in psychedelic sandstone. Head out to **White Domes**, past **Rainbow Vista** and the trailhead for **Fire Canyon** and **Silica Dome** (where Captain Kirk perished in *Star Trek: Generations*). **Atlatl Rock** has artistic petroglyphs.

INFORMATION
Location 30 miles (48km) southeast of Las Vegas
Getting there 🚗 From the Strip (45 minutes): I-15 south to I-215 east to I-515/US 93 and 95; at Boulder City, take US 93 east
Contact ☎ 702-494-2517, 866-730-9097; www.usbr.gov/lc/hooverdam
Costs Dam tours adult/child/concession $11/6/9, parking $7
When to go Visitor centers ☻ 8:30am to 4:30pm, dam tours ☻ 9am to 5:15pm

GRAND CANYON NATIONAL PARK

The **Grand Canyon** is the USA's best-known natural attraction. At 277 miles (446km) long, roughly 10 miles (16km) wide and one mile (1.6km) deep, it's an incredible spectacle of technicolor rock strata. When President Theodore Roosevelt visited in 1903, he sagely remarked, 'You cannot improve on it.'

The canyon's many peaks and buttes and its meandering rims give access to fantastic vistas. Descending into the canyon on hiking trails reveals a breathtaking variety in the landscape, wildlife and climate. Popular flightseeing day trips from Las Vegas (which are often combined with flyovers of Hoover Dam and Lake Mead, and a ground tour of the South Rim) introduce short-stay visitors to this stunning hole in the ground.

Although the canyon's rims are only 10 miles (16km) apart as the crow flies, it's a 215 mile (346km), five-hour drive on narrow roads between the South and North Rim visitor centers. If you want to feel like a pioneering explorer, consider skipping the congested **South Rim**, where there is no escaping the crowds during peak summer season. Though the South Rim receives over 90% of the four million people who visit the park each year, the **North Rim** is actually a little closer to Las Vegas, and it's a lot closer to Utah's gorgeous Zion and Bryce Canyon National Parks.

INFORMATION

Location 280 miles (450km) east of Las Vegas
Getting there 🚗 From the Strip (five hours): for South Rim, take I-15 south to I-215 east to US 93 south to I-40 east to AZ 64 north to Grand Canyon Village; North Rim is 265 miles (426km; about 4½ hours) from Las Vegas
Contact ☎ 928-638-7888; www.nps.gov/grca
Costs $20 per vehicle (good for seven days)
When to go South Rim 🕑 24/7/365; North Rim 🕑 mid-May to mid-October
Eating South Rim: El Tovar Dining Room, Arizona Room; North Rim: Grand Canyon Lodge Dining Room

RED ROCK CANYON

The 130-square-mile (337 sq-km) **Red Rock Canyon National Conservation Area** should be on everyone's must-see list, but fortunately it isn't. The startling contrast between the artificial neon glow of Las Vegas and the awesome natural forces of the canyon can't be exaggerated.

Created about 65 million years ago, the canyon is actually more like a valley, with a steep, rugged escarpment rising 3000ft (914m). A 13-mile (21-km), one-way **scenic loop** passes by its most striking natural features. Rugged hiking trails leading to seasonal waterfalls. The **Calico Hills** area is the premier place for sport rock climbing. Popular **Willow Springs** picnic area offers easy nature walks, including the trail to White Rock that leads past natural springs where you can observe desert wildlife.

Before reaching Red Rock, blink and you'll miss driving by the tiny, dusty town of Blue Diamond, where **McGhie's Bike Outpost** (☎ 702-875-4820; www.bikeoutpost.com) is a one-stop shop for mountain-bike rentals ($35 to $50 per day) and guided tours (from $109, including Las Vegas hotel pick-ups) around Red Rock Canyon, as well as 125 miles (201km) of single track in the Cottonwood Valley and Black Velvet areas.

Heading north on NV 159, hokey **Bonnie Springs**, the scene of countless B-movie shoots, is just a touristy sideshow for kiddies: Old West melodramas, simulated hangings and gunfights, miniature train rides, a wax museum, the works – don't even bother. Just up the road, **Spring Mountain Ranch State Park** (☎ 702-875-4141; http://parks.nv.gov/smr.htm; admission $5; ☼ 10am-4pm), once owned by 'The Aviator' Howard Hughes, is more authentic, not to mention more tranquil. Come for the shady picnic spots, walking paths, historical exhibits and guided tours.

INFORMATION

Location 20 miles (32km) west of Las Vegas
Getting there 🚗 From the Strip (30 minutes): I-15 south to Blue Diamond Rd (NV 160), then 10 miles to NV 159
Contact ☎ 702-515-5367; www.redrockcanyonlv.org
Costs $5/2 per car/bicycle
When to go Visitor center ☼ 8am to 4:30pm, scenic loop ☼ 6am to 5pm, to 7pm spring and fall, to 8pm summer
Eating Red Rock Casino Resort Spa (☎ 702-797-7576; 11011 W Charleston Blvd, at I-215)

Red Rock Canyon

TOUR OUTFITTERS

Hoover Dam package deals can save you ticketing headaches. Hour-long air tours of the Grand Canyon start around $100 per person; day-long air/ground combos run $225 to $275, and premier helicopter tours landing on the canyon's floor fetch over $350. Free Strip hotel pick-up and drop-off are included with most tours; check online for deep discounts. For city tours, see p168.

Adventure Las Vegas (☎ 869-9991, 888-846-4747; www.adventurelasvegas.com; tours $89-595; ☾ reservations 24hr) This one-stop shop for down-'n'-dirty adventure tours arranges everything from sunset horseback rides to soaring glider rides over the Las Vegas Valley to 4WD expeditions to Eldorado Canyon and Death Valley.

Black Canyon River Adventures (☎ 294-1414, 800-455-3490; www.blackcanyonad ventures.com; Hacienda Hotel & Casino, Boulder City; tours adult/concession $83/51 plus $33 transportation to & from Las Vegas) Take a three-hour motor-assisted raft journey down the Colorado River. Boats launch from the base of Hoover Dam and visit several hot springs en route to Willow Beach Marina.

Down River Outfitters (☎ 293-1190, 800-748-3702; www.downriveroutfitters.com; full-day tour $150, canoe/kayak rentals per person $45/55) Guided small-group kayak trips through Black Canyon, visiting hidden caves, waterfalls and hot springs. DIY canoe or kayak rentals include shuttles to the Hoover Dam launch site and pick-ups from Willow Beach.

Escape Adventures (☎ 596-2953, 800-596-2953; www.escapeadventures.com; half/full day from $89/149) Escape the city's neon jungle for a mountain-biking, road-cycling or hiking adventure in stunning Red Rock Canyon, or overnight trips to nearby national parks.

Papillon Grand Canyon Helicopters (☎ 736-7243, 888-635-7272; www.papillon.com; flights adult/child from $55/35; ☾ departures 8am-10:30pm) Vegas' original helicopter-flightseeing outfitter does luxury tours all over the Southwest. Its half-day 'Grand Canyon Celebration' is among the most popular tours.

Pink Jeep Tours (☎ 895-6777, 888-900-4480; www.pinkjeeplasvegas.com; half day $79-99, full day $119-326) Offers intimate off-road journeys to the Valley of Fire, Mt Charleston, Red Rock Canyon, Hoover Dam and Eldorado Canyon. The Grand Canyon Tour Combo includes short helicopter and pontoon-boat rides.

BACKGROUND

HISTORY

'What history?' you ask. Given what's left to see, you may be forgiven. Unlike the rest of the ruin-laden US Southwest, Las Vegas has only scarce traces of early history. The Uto-Aztecan–speaking Paiute tribe of Native Americans inhabited the Las Vegas Valley for a millennium before the Spanish Trail was blazed through this last area of the country to be explored by Europeans.

Contrary to Hollywood legend, there was much more at this dusty crossroads in the Mojave Desert than a few ramshackle gambling houses, tumbleweeds and cacti the day that mobster Benjamin 'Bugsy' Siegel rolled into this one-horse settlement and erected a glamorous, tropical themed casino under the searing sun.

TAMING THE FRONTIER

Amid the hard-scrabble legions of miners who arrived in the mid-19th century was a group of men hell-bent on doing God's work in Indian country. These Mormons were sent from Salt Lake City by leader Brigham Young to colonize the expanding state of Deseret, as they called their spiritual homeland. Their Las Vegas fort stood for only two years.

In 1905 the driving of a golden spike signaled the completion of a railroad linking Salt Lake City to Los Angeles. Thus Las Vegas, then known as Ragtown, entered the modern era. Small farms and ranches flourished throughout the Vegas Valley. Sin also took root in the infamous red-light district known as Block 16. Home to gambling, booze and prostitution, this row of saloons, with their makeshift 'cribs' out back, survived Nevada's 1911 ban on gambling and the supposedly 'dry' years of Prohibition.

BEST TOWN BY A DAM SITE

The federally sponsored Boulder (later named Hoover) Dam project and the legalization of gambling in 1931 carried Las Vegas through the Great Depression that followed the stock-market crash of 1929. Bookmakers fleeing Los Angeles and Tijuana, Mexico, flocked to the newly minted Sin City.

Top left Salesperson inside New York-New York (p49) **Top right** Getting cheeky **Bottom** 'Adult shops' on the streets of Vegas **Previous Page** On the streets of Vegas

BACKGROUND

Lax divorce requirements, quickie weddings, legalized prostitution and championship boxing bouts proved safe bets for local boosters. New Deal dollars kept flowing into Southern Nevada's coffers right through WWII, which brought a huge air-force base to town, plus a paved highway to LA.

THE FABULOUS FIFTIES

Along with the rest of America, post-WWII Las Vegas felt like a glorious boomtown again. Backed by East Coast mob money, gangster Benjamin 'Bugsy' Siegel opened the $6-million Flamingo hotel in 1946. With its incandescent pastel paint job, tuxedoed janitors, Hollywood entertainers and eight-story flashing neon-lit towers, it became the model for the new Las Vegas to come.

Soon after, the Cold War justified constructing the Nevada Test Site. Initially unconcerned about radiation fallout, Las Vegans took the atomic age in stride. Monthly above-ground atomic blasts shattered casino windows downtown while mushroom clouds rose on the horizon, and the city crowned a 'Miss Atomic Bomb' pin-up girl as its ambassador to the world.

FROM MOBSTERS TO MEGARESORTS

Big-name entertainers like Frank Sinatra, Liberace and Sammy Davis Jr arrived on stage at the same time as topless French showgirls, while mob-backed tycoons upped the casino-glitz ante. In the face of mounting bad publicity from notorious links to organized crime, the high-profile purchase of the Desert Inn in 1967 by eccentric billionaire Howard Hughes gave the gambling industry a much-needed patina of legitimacy.

WHERE HAVE ALL THE LOUNGE LIZARDS GONE?

In the heyday of Las Vegas lounge acts during the 1950s and early '60s, Rat Pack singers Frank Sinatra, Dean Martin and Sammy Davis Jr and their imitators would pack the casinos by attracting big gamblers. It was during those days that this two-bit Nevada railroad town was transformed into an entertainment mecca.

Sure, there were some flops, even back then: Elvis' first performance at the New Frontier in 1956 barely registered. But casino showrooms were still where all the action was. So, what happened? In the late 1960s casinos began knocking down the showroom walls in order to open them up to the gaming tables, and the stars left after they realized that audiences were now only paying half-attention.

Only a handful of casino showrooms have survived into the 21st century.

Spearheaded by Hughes' spending spree, corporate ownership of casinos blossomed and publicly traded companies bankrolled a building bonanza in the late 1960s and early '70s. The 1973 debut of the original MGM Grand, now the world's largest hotel, and the launch of Steve Wynn's fabulous Mirage casino hotel in 1989 signaled that the age of the corporate 'megaresort' had dawned.

A MODERN MECCA
The 1990s saw the building boom on the Strip get even bigger, as the Luxor's gigantic black pyramid arose from the desert, Treasure Island launched its pirate battles, the Stratosphere Tower became the tallest building in the western US, Paris-Las Vegas erected its ersatz Eiffel Tower and the Venetian's gondoliers started singing.

The 21st century started off with an even bigger bang, as Steve Wynn imploded the vintage Desert Inn, then spent five years crafting his eponymous megaresort. Today Las Vegas boasts all but a few of the world's 20 biggest hotels. As slot machines go cashless and omnipotent surveillance goes digital, the illusion of Sin City approaches the Orwellian dream-nightmare.

GOVERNMENT & POLITICS
In 1999, in a major blow to official public-relations efforts to clean up Sin City's image, Las Vegas voters elected long-time criminal defense lawyer Oscar Goodman to be their mayor. Goodman, who gained fame as a legal shark defending goodfellas like Frank 'Lefty' Rosenthal and Tony 'The Ant' Spillotro, had even portrayed himself in the movie *Casino*. Goodman also devoted much of his practice to the poor and the dispossessed, often working pro bono. In 1998 he won the release from prison of a cancer-ridden woman who had murdered her abusive husband – a noble thing in the minds of many.

The alleged 'barrister to butchers,' as an editorial in the *Las Vegas Review-Journal* described him, makes no effort to hide his past. Indeed, the purported 'mouthpiece

DID YOU KNOW?
> 39 million tourists visited Las Vegas in 2006
> The Las Vegas Valley has over 130,000 hotel rooms
> Annual gambling revenue nears $8.5 billion
> The cost of living in Las Vegas is lower than in any other US metro area

of the mafia' loves to talk about the old days. But he caught the voters' fancy with a populist platform calling for developers to pay fees to help solve the city's traffic and pollution woes. Goodman's more notorious achievements include getting his mug on a limited-edition gambling chip, being a guest celebrity photographer for *Playboy*, endorsing a brand of gin for $100,000 (donated to charities) and hosting 'Martini with the Mayor' nights. Viva Las Vegas!

After being re-elected with 86% of the vote in 2003, Goodman is still enjoying enormous popularity. He frequently uses the mayoral pulpit for fiery comments on hot-button political issues, such as storing nuclear waste at Yucca Mountain, that may fall outside the scope of municipal government but are always on the minds of Las Vegans. Goodman has also been a tireless proponent of the need to redevelop the downtown urban core. He'll be a tough act for the next mayor to follow in 2007.

ENVIRONMENT

Las Vegas is an environmentalist's nightmare, the antithesis of a naturalist's vision of America. Ironically, it's also the gateway to some of the Southwest's most spectacular natural attractions, such as the Grand Canyon.

Water usage is the chief concern. The city of Las Vegas (Spanish for 'the meadows') receives the vast majority of its water from the Colorado River, which feeds Lake Mead. Projections suggest that the Vegas Valley may exhaust its entire water supply by 2022. What will happen when the aquifers run dry is anyone's guess.

Air pollution is an equally vexing topic: the valley is fringed by mountains that trap hazardous particles, and the city is in near-constant

---

NEVADA'S NUCLEAR DESERT

The US government stopped exploding nuclear bombs underground at the Nevada Test Site in 1992, but a nuclear future still looms large for state residents. The US Department of Energy report has been pushing for Yucca Mountain as the best location for the nation's only long-term radioactive nuclear-waste repository.

Did we say long-term? The proposed site, which would eventually hold 77,000 tons of used spent nuclear fuel, would remain deadly for 300,000 years. In that time, the earth itself may experience an ice age, and Yucca Mountain, currently one of the driest and most remote places in the lower 48 states, may no longer be a desert.

Anyone care to predict the weather a few millennia from now?

---

violation of federal air-quality standards. On most days the sky harbors a dirty inversion layer, sometimes so thick that the mountains are invisible. With traffic on the freeways and at McCarran International Airport on the rise, it's looking a lot like LA.

LIFE IN LAS VEGAS

Infamous historically for its mob ties, Sin City's bad reputation precedes, overwhelms and obscures its day-to-day reality. Known as America's dirty little secret, Nevada's biggest metropolis today sells itself to visitors with the naughty slogan 'What happens in Vegas, stays in Vegas.'

All of that belies what is, at heart, a conservative cow town. Prostitution, all images to the contrary, is illegal in Clark County. Gay and lesbian life is often hidden, remaining underground to avoid the wrath of the religious right. Racism has a long history in Southern Nevada, too, and it wasn't until the 1960s that the color line was first crossed at Las Vegas' casino hotels

The vast majority of Las Vegans were born outside the state. Half of city residents ticked 'white,' nearly a quarter claimed Hispanic heritage and 10% checked African American in the 2000 US census. Asians, Native Americans and Pacific Islanders (including a surprising number of transplanted Hawaiians) comprise the bulk of the rest of a rapidly growing minority population. It's often noted that over 5000 people move to Las Vegas every month; what's less often reported is that another few thousand throw in the towel each month and leave. With so many new folks coming and going all the time, a disturbingly transient feeling permeates the city.

Lady Luck does not smile on everyone here. Las Vegas has been ranked as the 'meanest city in America' in which to be homeless. If you wander east of Fremont St or into the so-called 'Naked City' between downtown and the Strip, it won't take five minutes before you'll run into someone desperately in need of help: a crack whore looking to score, a babbling schizophrenic pushing a shopping cart full of garbage bags or a degenerate gambler drunk off a 40oz beer can stuffed in a crumpled paper bag.

Cultural arts in Las Vegas – like clean government in Chicago, sizzling nightlife in Salt Lake City or real breasts in LA – would, until recently, have been just another urban oxymoron. However, that's no longer the case, thanks to a thriving art scene that has sprung up.

GIRLS! GIRLS! GIRLS!

Prostitution was banned from Las Vegas in the 1940s, when the US military forced the closure of the city's brothels. But Mayor Oscar Goodman has gone on record with his pro-prostitution stance, saying that legalizing prostitution here would 'turn old motels into beautiful brothels,' and speculating about how Fremont St might be advantageously turned out into becoming Nevada's Little Amsterdam.

And then there's George Flint, an ordained minister who is Nevada's only paid lobbyist for the state's legal bordellos. His job is to see that attempts to end legal prostitution in Nevada, where it is still permitted in 10 of the state's 17 counties, don't get too far.

That said, 'full-service Barbie girls' and 'barely legal Asian playmates' are not what the conservative moral majority of Southern Nevadans want to see in their own backyards.

Las Vegas is still a city of die-hard sports fans, and there are scores of race and sports books inside casinos to prove it. The problem is, there aren't any professional home teams to root for. Most of the betting action is placed on national franchise teams, although UNLV college sports are big business. Monday Night Football is huge at bars all over town. Everyone gets revved up for 'Fight Night,' too, when championship boxing matches are staged.

DOS & DON'TS

Sure it's service-oriented culture by mandate, but everywhere you go people will stop and say hello, and ask if they can help. Polite requests will solve any problems you may have faster than noisy complaints.

The legal age for drinking and gambling is 21. You can buy booze everywhere 24/7. If you look under 35, always carry ID, especially for getting into bars and nightclubs. Open containers of alcohol are illegal in public but often overlooked, except in vehicles. Cops crack down on DUI (driving under the influence, whether of alcohol or drugs) with a vengeance; fines and sentences are as stiff as the casinos' free drinks are watered down. More people are injured in crosswalks than in auto accidents. Play the smart odds and take a cab.

Smoking cancer sticks is permissible anywhere; stogie puffing is restricted. Unlike in California, nonsmoking sections are rarely divided off at restaurants. Hotels advertise nonsmoking guest rooms, but there are no guarantees – you may sniff more than a whiff of cigarettes inside 'em. One comedian says he loves Vegas because he can savor a cigar in a hospital elevator – full of pregnant women!

When movie stars first landed in Las Vegas in the 1950s, no lady would be caught dead in anything less than an evening gown once the cocktail hour arrived, and even off-duty showgirls dressed like starlets. Meanwhile, Sy Devore tailored European-style suits for the Rat Pack and even the janitors wore tuxedos at the Flamingo casino hotel. Nostalgic locals lament that T-shirts and jeans are the new norm. Today dress codes exist only at high-end restaurants and exclusive bars and nightclubs.

FURTHER READING

Contemporary nonfiction books about Vegas tend to focus on one topic: beating the casinos at their game. Few famous authors have hit the jackpot in Vegas, but gonzo journalist Hunter S Thompson (*Fear and Loathing in Las Vegas*), 1960s countercultural narrator Tom Wolfe (*The Kandy-Kolored Tangerine-Flake Streamline Baby*), pop novelist and screenwriter Mario Puzo (*Inside Las Vegas*) and rock critic Richard Meltzer have all confronted the underbelly of the shimmering beast.

Scores of pulpy biographies have been written about the gangsters, movie stars and entertainers who pushed this dusty Nevada town into the spotlight, from gangster Bugsy Siegel to Elvis and beyond. *Rat Pack Confidential: Frank, Dean, Sammy, Peter, Joey and the Last Great Show Biz Party* by Shawn Levy has a swingin' style that echoes the hip stylings of the era, plus dishes all the dirt on the celebrities of Vegas' golden age.

Nicholas Pileggi's *Casino: Love and Honor in Las Vegas* tracks the true-crime story of the Chicago mafia's move to take over Vegas, with all the bribery, book-making, mistresses and shootings in the dead of night leading in a downward spiral to disaster. Think all of the mobsters have left town and Vegas has been Disneyfied? Think again. *The Money and the Power: The Making of Las Vegas and Its Hold on America* by Sally Denton and Roger Morris is a haunting investigation of the city's underworld.

Running Scared: The Life and Treacherous Times of Las Vegas Casino King Steve Wynn, by local newspaper reporter John L Smith, was so racy and controversial that Wynn sued and bankrupted its original publisher.

In *Skin City: Uncovering the Las Vegas Sex Industry*, long-time resident Jack Sheehan interviews madams, strippers and XXX-film stars for a scandalous tell-all exposé. *Brothel: Mustang Ranch and Its Women* by Alexa Albert is a conflicted, highly personalized account of the last days of Nevada's most famous cathouse. *Cult Vegas: The Weirdest! The Wildest! The Swingin'est Town on Earth* by Mike Weatherford, an entertainment

VINTAGE VEGAS SOUNDTRACK
> 'Luck Be a Lady,' as recorded by Frank Sinatra
> 'You're Nobody Till Somebody Loves You,' as recorded by Dean Martin
> 'Viva Las Vegas,' as recorded by Elvis Presley
> 'I've Got You Under My Skin,' as recorded by Keely Smith and Louis Prima
> 'Ace in the Hole,' as recorded by Bobby Darin

...or just about anything from Capitol Records' *The Rat Pack: Live at the Sands* album or the *Live from Las Vegas* series. For a red-light burlesque groove, the rare *Las Vegas Grind* series from Crypt Records (www.cryptrecords.com) should satisfy your all of your bad-girl urges.

reporter for the *Las Vegas Review-Journal*, reveals all the offbeat trivia and celebrity gossip you could ever want to know.

For high-culture vultures, the landmark 1995 anthology *Literary Las Vegas: The Best Writing about America's Most Fabulous City*, edited by Mike Tronnes, excerpts essays and short stories spanning 40 years, from atomic bomb–viewing picnics to the wedding-chapel industry. Robert Venturi's classic *Learning from Las Vegas* was the first to celebrate the city's architecture as pop art, and *Viva Las Vegas: After-Hours Architecture* by Alan Hess is a lushly illustrated history of pre-Luxor properties.

FILM & TV

Often said to be the only city in the world with a more distorted sense of reality than Los Angeles, Vegas has long been a favorite shooting location for Hollywood.

Casino interiors were cast often by the industry in the 1940s, when Frank Sinatra made his silver-screen debut and movie mogul Howard Hughes frequently worked on location. Atomic testing captured the imagination of B-grade sci-fi directors in the 1950s. Sinatra's Rat Pack enjoyed frequent cameos, especially after their hijinks in the classic *Ocean's 11* (1960), and Elvis shook his thang in *Viva Las Vegas* (1964). James Bond glorified glitzy Vegas in *Diamonds are Forever* (1971), while the epic *Godfather* (1972), written by self-described 'degenerate gambler' Mario Puzo, was the first flick to portray the Mafia in Las Vegas. Martin Scorsese delved deeper into 'the organization' with *Casino* (1995).

In *Rain Man* (1988), Dustin Hoffman and Tom Cruise conspired to beat the house edge. In *Bugsy* (1991), Warren Beatty and Annette Benning bring to life the original Flamingo casino hotel. Robert Redford gives Demi Moore a booty call – to the dismay of her on-screen hubby Woody Harrelson – in the drama *Indecent Proposal* (1993). Obviously infatuated with Sin City, Nicholas Cage starred with Sarah Jessica Parker in *Honeymoon in Vegas* (1992) and Elizabeth Shue in the brutal *Leaving Las Vegas* (1995). The epitome of bad taste, Chevy Chase's *Vegas Vacation* (1997) nevertheless had a few redeeming moments, including those with Wayne Newton and Siegfried and Roy on stage at the Mirage.

No movie rebirthed the contemporary cool of Vegas as much as *Swingers* (1996) did. The cinematic success of Hunter S Thompson's classic *Fear and Loathing in Las Vegas* (1998), starring Johnny Depp and Benicio Del Toro, confirmed that sin was in once again. In a remake of the Sinatra classic *Ocean's Eleven* (2001), a star-studded cast including Brad Pitt, George Clooney and Julia Roberts plots to bilk a string of casinos. The independent flick *The Cooler* (2003), featuring William H Macy as a no-luck gambler and Alec Baldwin as a casino mogul with anger management issues, is all aces.

The megahit prime-time TV show *CSI: Crime Scene Investigation* sets fictionalized police forensic investigations against the backdrop of Vegas' neon glow, with a cast of characters that includes a former exotic dancer and a gambling addict. Reality TV hit Las Vegas like an epidemic, too, starting with MTV's *Real World: Las Vegas* in the 1990s. More recent was *The Entertainer*, an unholy hybrid of *American Idol* and *The Apprentice*, but starring genial Wayne Newton instead of grumpy Donald Trump.

DIRECTORY
TRANSPORTATION
ARRIVAL & DEPARTURE
AIR

Las Vegas is served by McCarran International Airport, just a crapshoot from the south end of the Strip, as well as a few smaller general aviation facilities around the city.

McCarran International Airport

McCarran (LAS; ☎ 261-5211; www.mccarran.com) is among the USA's 10 busiest airports. Baggage handling is notoriously slow, but self-service kiosks ease check-in headaches. Most domestic airlines use Terminal 1; international, charter and some domestic flights depart from Terminal 2. A free tram links outlying gates. There are ATMs, a full-service bank, 24-hour fitness center, first-aid and police stations, free wi-fi internet access and slot machines. The left-luggage lockers are not available for use.

Taxi & Limousine

Taxi fares to Strip hotels (allow at least 30 minutes in heavy traffic) are $10 to $20, cash only; fares to downtown average $15 to $25. 'Long-hauling' through the airport connector tunnel is common; tell your driver to use the Paradise Rd surface route instead unless time is of the essence. From the airport, it costs $41 per hour for a chartered sedan, $48 for a six-person stretch limousine.

Shuttle

Notoriously slow 24-hour airport shuttles charge $5 per person to the Strip, $6.50 to downtown or off-Strip hotels.

Bus

If you're traveling light, CAT's bus 108 runs between 5am and 2am

---

CLIMATE CHANGE & TRAVEL

Travel – especially air travel – is a significant contributor to global climate change. At Lonely Planet, we believe that all who travel have a responsibility to limit their personal impact. As a result, we have teamed with Rough Guides and other concerned industry partners to support Climate Care, which allows people to offset the greenhouse gases they are responsible for with contributions to energy-saving projects and other climate-friendly initiatives in the developing world. Lonely Planet offsets all staff and author travel.

For more information, turn to the responsible travel pages on www.lonelyplanet .com. For details on offsetting your carbon emissions and a carbon calculator, go to www .climatecare.org.

from the airport to the convention center and Sahara monorail station ($1.25, 25 minutes). Bus 109 runs 24/7 between the airport and the Downtown Transportation Center ($1.25, 35 to 55 minutes), a short walk from Fremont St casino hotels.

CAR & MOTORCYCLE

If they're not flying, most visitors drive to Las Vegas. It's about a four-hour drive (270 miles; 435km) from Los Angeles, five hours (330 miles; 530km) from San Diego and nine hours (570 miles; 920km) from San Francisco. Expect serious delays on weekends and holidays. For recorded updates on road conditions, dial ☎ 877-687-6237 for Nevada, ☎ 800-427-7623 for California.

TRAVEL DOCUMENTS

Foreign visitors must have a machine-readable passport that has biometric identifiers and is valid for at least six months beyond their planned exit date. Canadians entering overland (though not by air) need only proof of citizenship with photo ID, but this is expected to change as early as January 1, 2008.

VISA

Visas are not required for citizens of the reciprocal 27 Visa Waiver Program (VWP) countries (including Australia, Ireland, New Zealand, the UK and many other European nations), who may enter the USA for up to 90 days visa-free. Everyone not covered by the visa-waiver exemption, and those wishing to stay longer, must wrangle a visa from a US embassy or consulate. Double-check the mercurial requirements at http://travel.state.gov.

RETURN/ONWARD TICKET

Travelers under the reciprocal visa-waiver program need round-trip or onward tickets to enter the US. Travelers applying for visas overseas will generally require such tickets as proof of their intent to return home.

GETTING AROUND

Las Vegas traffic is often gridlocked and the most heavily touristed areas are flat, so the best way to get around is on foot, in combination with occasional taxi, monorail or bus rides. In this book, the nearest monorail station (M) or bus route (🚌) is noted after each listing by the relevant icon.

BUS

Citizens Area Transit (CAT; ☎ 228-7433, 800-228-3911; www.catride.com) operates from 5:30am to 1:30am daily, with the most popular Strip and

DIRECTORY

downtown routes running 24/7. The fare is $1.25 ($2 for double-decker Deuce buses along Las Vegas Blvd); exact change is required. Free maps and timetables are available from drivers and at the **Downtown Transportation Center** (Map pp184–5, C3; 300 N Casino Center Blvd).

Many off-Strip casino hotels offer limited free shuttle-bus services to/from the Strip.

CAR & MOTORCYCLE

If you've got your own set of wheels, free valet (tip $2) and/or self-parking is available almost everywhere on the Strip. Parking is tighter downtown, but all casino hotels have lots or garages that are free with validation. Traffic usually moves slowly, especially during weekday rush hours or on weekends along the Strip. Listen to KNUU 'K-News' (970AM) for traffic and weather updates every 10 minutes. Gas costs less than $3 per US gallon.

Economy car-rental rates start at around $25 per day or $135 per week, plus $10 to $15 per day for insurance (usually optional). Ferraris and exotic convertibles fetch $200 to $1000 per day. Expect to pay sales taxes of up to 7.5%, governmental-service fees of 10%, a customer facility charge ($3 per day) and 10% airport surcharge. For weekends, reserve at least two weeks in advance.

Agencies with airport desks include **Alamo** (☎ 800-462-5266; www .alamo.com), **Budget** (☎ 800-922-2899; www.budgetvegas.com) and **Thrifty** (☎ 800-847-4389; www.thrifty.com). In most instances, rental cars can be delivered to your hotel. For something glamorous, ring **Rent-A-Vette** (Map pp190–1, C6; ☎ 736-2592, 800-372-1981; www.rent-a-vette.com; 5021 Swenson St). **Las Vegas Motorcycle Rentals** (Map pp190–1, E1; ☎ 431-8500, 877-571-7174; www.lvhd.com; 2605 S Eastern Ave) rents a range of brand-new Harleys, from Sportsters ($90 per day) to Fat Boys ($155 per day), including unlimited mileage, a helmet and rain suit.

MONORAIL & TRAM

A private **monorail system** (☎ 699-8299; www.lvmonorail.com; ⌚ 7am-2am Mon-Thu, to 3am Fri-Sun) links properties along the Strip's resort corridor, shuttling between the MGM Grand, Bally's, the Flamingo, Harrah's, the convention center, the Hilton and the Sahara. One-way rides cost $5; multi-ride discounts are available.

A free private tram system connects TI (Treasure Island) and the Mirage; and Excalibur, Luxor and Mandalay Bay. At press time, the tram between the Bellagio and Monte Carlo was under reconstruction.

TAXI

Fares (cash only) are metered: flagfall is $3.20 plus $2 per mile, or 40¢ per minute for waiting. A 4½-mile lift from one end of the Strip to the other runs $10 to $15, plus tip. Taxi stands are at every casino and hotel entrance. Reputable companies include **Desert Cab** (☎ 386-9102), **Western** (☎ 736-8000) and **Yellow/Checker/Star** (☎ 873-2000). Any complaints can be filed via http://taxi.state.nv.us.

TRAVEL PASSES

Monorail passes cost $15/40 for a one-/three-day ticket, or $35 for a 10-ride pass. CAT's 24-hour bus pass costs $5.

TROLLEY

Private air-con **trolleys** (☎ 382-1404) ply the length of the Strip, detouring to the Hilton on Paradise Rd. Frequent stops make these the slowest way to get around. Trolleys operate every 15 to 20 minutes daily, 9:30am to 1:30am. The fare is $2 (day pass $5); exact change is required.

ACCOMMODATIONS

Vegas hits the jackpot here, with a grand total of over 130,000 guest rooms. Even if a bankroll isn't burning a hole in your pocket, a little luxury can be had more cheaply here than almost anywhere else in the world. Of course an exquisite penthouse villa overlooking the Strip, with perks like 24-hour butler service, still costs $10,000 per night.

On your first trip to Vegas, almost any casino hotel on the Strip will bedazzle, but don't go by name recognition only. Some famous hotels on the North Strip have the most disappointing rooms and location. The Center Strip is where the hot action is, and you'll pay for it. The South Strip is a perfect compromise:

Need a place to stay? Find and book it at lonelyplanet .com. More than 40 properties are featured for Las Vegas – each personally visited, thoroughly reviewed and happily recommended by a Lonely Planet author. From hostels to high-end hotels, we've hunted out the places that will bring you unique and special experiences. Read independent reviews by authors and other travelers, and get practical information including amenities, maps and photos. Then reserve your room simply and securely via Haystack – our online booking service. It's all at www.lonelyplanet.com/accommodation.

haystack.lonelyplanet.com

LAS VEGAS' BEST HOTELS
Best Hip Hotels
> Hard Rock (www.hardrockhotel.com)
> Palms (www.palms.com)
> Red Rock (www.redrocklasvegas.com)
> THEHotel at Mandalay Bay (www.thehotelatmandalaybay.com)
> Wynn (www.wynnlasvegas.com)

Best-Value Theme Hotels
> Luxor (www.luxor.com)
> MGM Grand (www.mgmgrand.com)
> New York-New York (www.nynyhotelcasino.com)
> Rio (www.harrahs.com/our_casinos/rlv)
> TI (Treasure Island; www.treasureisland.com)

Best for Extravagant Luxury
> Bellagio (www.bellagio.com)
> Caesars Palace (www.caesarspalace.com)
> THEHotel at Mandalay Bay (www.thehotelatmandalaybay.com)
> Venetian (www.venetian.com)
> Wynn (www.wynnlasvegas.com)

Best for Low Rollers
> Golden Nugget (www.goldennugget.com)
> Las Vegas Hilton (www.lvhilton.com)
> Orleans (www.orleanscasino.com)
> Sahara (www.saharavegas.com)
> Stratosphere (www.stratospherehotel.com)

you'll get the full-on Vegas experience, but almost always for less. Downtown is mostly for local gamblers and penny-pinching visitors who've tired of the Strip scene. Outlying area hotels offer some deals, if you're willing to make the drive.

Whatever you do, don't arrive without a reservation. It's amazing how often every hotel in town is booked solid. Year-round, room rates average 50% less Sunday through Thursday nights. Unless you're on a junket yourself, avoid visiting during the biggest conventions, when hotel rates shoot sky-high. The slowest times of year are during the hot summer months (June, July and August) and between Thanksgiving and Christmas. If you're claustrophobic, pass on New Year's Eve and other major holidays (p166). Contact the Las Vegas Convention & Visitors Authority (LVCVA; p169) about last-minute specials and for current convention dates.

Many properties lure customers during slow periods with discounted room rates, most easily found on the hotels' own websites or at online travel discounters like www.travelworm.com. Know that Strip properties can offer rooms for the same price as a dumpy downtown joint since they make their bucks in gaming areas, whereas the dumpy joint doesn't have a casino to recoup its losses.

If you're looking for a lower rate that's unavailable or you want to stay at a hotel that's sold out, check back in a few days or a week or two. Sometimes you can suddenly reserve rooms for much less than you'd been quoted before. It also pays to check with the hotel where you'll be staying a week or so in advance to see if the rates you were quoted when you booked have changed. If they've fallen, request that your reserved rate be lowered, too.

PRACTICALITIES

BUSINESS HOURS

Open 24/7/365 is the rule at casino hotels. Normal business hours are weekdays 9am to 5pm. Some post offices stay open later and on weekends. Banks usually keep shorter hours, though some branches are open Saturday morning. Retail shopping hours are 10am to 9pm (to 6pm Sunday); casino shops stay open until 11pm or later. Christmas is one of the few holidays on which most non-casino businesses close.

DISCOUNTS

The biggest discounts are 'comps' handed out by casinos to members of slot clubs and 'rated' gamblers. 'Full RFB' (room, food and board) is the coveted treatment lavished on the highest rollers (aka 'whales'). Casino 'fun books,' usually given only to guests but sometimes available just for the asking, get you a range of discounts, starting with a free souvenir from the gift shop. Free printable coupons are available at websites such as www.vegas4locals.com, www.lasvegasinsider.com and www.lasvegasfunbook.com.

Freebie magazines distributed in most hotel rooms are the source of the biggest discounts (often half-price or two-for-one admission) on shows, dinner and attractions.

DIRECTORY

Seniors (over 50 in many cases) and children may receive small discounts at many attractions and some restaurants.

ELECTRICITY

North American plugs have two or three pins (usually two flat pins, often with a round 'grounding' pin). Adaptors for European plugs are available, but travelers from Asia and Australia should bring their own.

EMERGENCIES

On the Strip and in downtown, beware of pickpockets working the crowds. Police and private security officers are out in force in casino hotels, and surveillance cameras are omnipresent. Utilize the in-room safes provided at most hotels and never leave your valuables unattended. Anywhere off Fremont St downtown, keep your wits about you.

For emergencies:

Police, fire, ambulance (☎ 911)
Police (nonemergency; ☎ 311, 229-3111)
Rape Crisis Hotline (☎ 366-1640)

For minor ailments and injuries, it's less expensive to go to a walk-in clinic than a hospital emergency room. Just east of the Strip, **Harmon Medical Center** (Map p182, C3; ☎ 796-1116; 150 E Harmon Ave; ☾ 24hr) offers courtesy vans and translation services. Emergency contraception services are available without a prescription from **Planned Parenthood** (Map pp178-9, G4; ☎ 878-7776; 3220 W Charleston Blvd; ☎ 547-9888; Suite 54, 3320 E Flamingo Rd).

HOLIDAYS

Holidays marked with an asterisk (*) are widely observed; some are observed the following Monday, if they fall on a weekend.

New Year's Day * 1 January
Martin Luther King Jr Day Third Monday in January
Presidents' Day Third Monday in February
Easter Sunday March/April
Memorial Day * Last Monday in May
Independence Day * 4 July
Labor Day * First Monday in September
Columbus Day Second Monday in October
Veterans' Day 11 November
Thanksgiving Day * Fourth Thursday in November
Christmas Day * 25 December

INTERNET

Most hotels have business centers that charge an arm and a leg for 24/7 internet access, but wireless is spreading like wildfire. The best free wi-fi hotspots are off-Strip at the convention center and airport. High-speed cable access in hotel rooms typically costs $10 per 24 hours; WebTV keyboards may be provided. Most hotels also have phones with data ports for dial-up ISP access, but may charge $1 or more per local call (30-minute limit).

The Lonely Planet website (www.lonelyplanet.com) offers a speedy link to many Sin City websites. Other informative and entertaining spots to surf:

LVCVA (www.visitlasvegas.com)
VEGAS.com (www.vegas.com)
Cheapo Vegas (www.cheapovegas.com)
LV Rocks (www.lvrocks.com)
Vegas Talk Radio (www.vegastalkradio.com)
Las Vegas Advisor (www.lasvegasadvisor.com)

Convenient cybercafés:
Cyber Stop (Map p182, C3; ☎ 736-4782; Hawaiian Marketplace, 3743 Las Vegas Blvd S; per 30min/1hr $8/12; ⏰ 8-2am)
FedEx/Kinkos (Map pp190-1; ☎ 951-2400; 395 Hughes Center Dr; per min 20¢; ⏰ 24/7/365) T-Mobile wi-fi hotspot.
FedEx/Kinkos (Map pp186-7, D2; ☎ 383-7022; 830 S 4th St; per min 20¢; ⏰ 8am-9pm Mon-Thu, 7am-10pm Fri) T-Mobile wi-fi hotspot.

MONEY

Casinos exist to separate you from your dough and will facilitate that end any way they can. Transaction fees at ATMs inside gaming areas are high ($3 or more). To avoid surcharges, use your debit card to get cash back when making purchases at select non-casino businesses. Casino hotel fees to exchange foreign currency are higher than at banks but lower than at most exchange bureaus. **American Express** (Map p180, B5; ☎ 739-8474; 2nd fl,

Fashion Show Mall, 3200 Las Vegas S; ⏰ 9am-9pm Mon-Fri, 10am-8pm Sat, 11am-6pm Sun) changes currencies at competitive rates. For exchange rates, see the Quick Reference page inside the front cover of this book.

The average visitor's gambling budget is $500 for their entire trip. How much you spend on a daily basis is entirely up to you. Accommodations will be your biggest expense, and hotel room rates go up and down like the stock market (see p163). Meals cost at least $10, though they could easily run over $100 per person. For more tips about saving money on attractions, dining and entertainment, see p165.

NEWSPAPERS & MAGAZINES

Nevada's largest daily newspaper is the conservative daily *Las Vegas Review Journal* (www.lvrj.com), which publishes jointly on Sunday with the tabloid *Las Vegas Sun* (www.lasvegassun.com); look for the former's Friday *Neon* entertainment guide. Free alternative weekly newspapers include *Las Vegas Weekly* (www.lasvegasweekly.com) and *CityLife* (www.lvcitylife.com). The glossy monthly magazine *Casino Player* (www.casinoplayer.com) targets gaming enthusiasts. Hotel rooms provide complimentary copies of industry promo magazines, such as *What's On* and *Showbiz Weekly*, which provide discount coupons.

ORGANIZED TOURS

Gray Line (☎ 384-1234, 800-634-6579; www.grayline.com) runs the most popular night-time city bus tour, which lasts six hours ($43); stops include the Bellagio's fountains and the Fremont Street Experience.

Papillon Grand Canyon Helicopters (☎ 736-7243, 888-635-7272; www.papillon.com), Vegas' original helicopter-flightseeing outfitter, is popular for its 10-minute 'Neon Nights Express' jetcopter flyovers of the Strip (from $55).

Bally's **Backstage Tour** (☎ 967-4567; tickets $10-15; ⌚ 11am Mon, Wed & Sat) takes you behind the scenes of Vegas' long-running $50-million showgirl revue, *Jubilee!*

Most folks are disappointed by the campy sideshow that starts off **Haunted Vegas Tours** (☎ 737-5540; www.hauntedvegastours.com; Greek Isles, 305 Convention Center Dr; tickets $47-58), but the after-dark bus trip around Sin City keeps 'em awake, thanks to an energetic guide who spins yarns about the ghost of Liberace creeping around Tivoli Gardens and gangster Bugsy Siegel haunting the Flamingo casino hotel.

For out-of-town guided trips, including to the Grand Canyon and Hoover Dam, see the boxed text, p148.

PHOTOGRAPHY & VIDEO

Print film is widely available, while digital memory cards and sticks are hard to find. **Millennium Foto** (Map p180, B6; ☎ 696-9430; Carnaval Court, 3475 Las Vegas Blvd S; ⌚ 9am-midnight) sells photographic supplies and offers digital photo printing and CD-burning services. Photographing in casinos is strongly discouraged and is prohibited at McCarran Airport.

If you purchase a video, note that the USA uses the NTSC color TV standard, which is not compatible with international standards like PAL and Secam.

TELEPHONE

The USA uses a variety of cellular-phone systems, most of which are incompatible with the GSM 900/1800 standard used throughout Europe, Asia and Africa. Most North American visitors can use their phones in Vegas, but check with your carrier about roaming charges before you start racking up minutes. On the Strip, Cyber Stop (p166) rents Nokia handsets (from $5 per day plus at least 85¢ per minute for calls). Using cell phones near casino race and sports books is prohibited.

Public phones are mostly coin-operated; some accept credit cards or have dataports for laptop and PDA internet access. Local calls generally cost 35¢. If calling a long-distance number outside the ☎ 702 area code, dial ☎ 1 first. Pharmacies and convenience stores sell prepaid phonecards, but they can be rip-offs – check the fine print for hidden fees and surcharges. Major carriers like **AT&T** (☎ 800-321-0288) can facilitate long-distance calls. See the inside front cover of this book for area codes.

USEFUL PHONE NUMBERS
Operator (☎ 0)
Collect (reverse-charge; ☎ 0)
International Operator (☎ 00)
International Direct Dial Code (☎ 011)
Local Directory Inquiries (☎ 411)
Time & Weather (☎ 248-4800)

TIPPING
Casino and hotel staff rely on tips to bring their incomes up to decent levels, while fortunes have been made by valet-parking concession owners. However, you should only withhold tips in cases of exceptionally poor service. See the inside front cover of this guidebook for advice on who to tip, and how much.

TOURIST INFORMATION
Many tour operators push unofficial 'visitor information,' but there's only one official city tourism office. **Las Vegas Convention & Visitors Authority** (LVCVA; Map pp190–1, B2;

☎ 892-7575, 877-847-4858; www.visitlasvegas.com; 3150 Paradise Rd; ☀ office 8am-5pm, toll-free hotline 6am-9pm).

The **Nevada Commission on Tourism** (☎ 800-638-2328; www.travelnevada.com) runs Nevada Welcome Centers:
Boulder City (☎ 294-1252; off US93; ☀ 8am-4:30pm) Near Hoover Dam.
Primm (☎ 874-1360; off I-15 exit 1; ☀ 9:30am-6:30pm) At the California state line; free email access (20 minutes) with out-of-state ID.

TRAVELERS WITH DISABILITIES
Vegas has the most ADA-accessible guestrooms in the USA. Wheelchair seating is widely available and assisted listening devices are offered at most showrooms. Most public transport and several hotel pools are lift-equipped. Unless otherwise noted, all attractions in this book are wheelchair-accessible. Guide dogs may be brought into restaurants, hotels and businesses. By law, all taxi companies must have a wheelchair-accessible van. If you're driving, bring your disabled-parking placard from home or apply for a 90-day temporary permit from **City Hall** (Map pp184–5, C4; ☎ 229-6431; 400 E Stewart Ave). For more info, contact the LVCVA's ADA coordinator at ☎ 892-7575 (voice relay ☎ 800-326-6888, TTY ☎ 800-326-6868).

>INDEX

See also separate subindexes for Casinos (p173), See (p173), Shop (p174), Eat (p174) and Play (p176).

A

accommodation 163-5
   hotels 164
   internet resources 163, 165
adult toys 87-8, *see also* Shop *subindex*
air travel 160-1
ambulance 166
arcades 80-2, *see also* Shop *subindex*
art galleries 66-8, *see also* See *subindex*
arts 155
Atlatl Rock 144
ATMs 167

B

baccarat 36
bachelor & bachelorette parties 132
Bally's 54
bars 120-3, *see also* Play *subindex*
Bellagio 38
Binion's 45
blackjack 36
Bonnie Springs 146
books 157-8, *see also* Shop *subindex*
buffets 13, 93
Bugsy Siegel 46, 152
bus travel 161-2
business hours 165

C

Caesars Palace 39
Calico Hills 146

California 54
car travel 161, 162
casinos 14, 32-61, *see also* Casinos *subindex*
   high limit 14
   low limit 18-19, 55
   retro 16-17
cell phones 168
cinemas 141-2, *see also* Play *subindex*
Circus Circus 54
clothing 82-3, *see also* Shop *subindex*
clubs, *see* nightclubs
comedy shows 139-41, *see also* Play *subindex*
contraception 166
costs 167
   food 91
craps 36
culture 155-7

D

disabilities, travelers with 169
discounts 165-6
Downtown 9, **184-5**
drinking 120-3, *see also* Play *subindex*

E

Eastside 9, **190-1**
El Cortez 54-5
electricity 166
Elvis impersonators 16, 24, 74, 75, 77
emergencies 166

entertainment 119-42, *see also* Play *subindex*
   tickets 119
environmental issues 154-5
events 127
Excalibur 55
exchange rates, *see inside front cover*

F

festivals 127
film 158-9
   festivals 127
Fire Canyon 144
fire services 166
Flamingo 46
food 13, 91-117, *see also* Eat *subindex*
   buffets 13, 93
   costs 91
free sights 31, 71
Fruit Loop 9

G

galleries 66-8
gambling 14, 32-61, *see also* casinos
gardens 72-5, *see also* See *subindex*
Gateway Arts District 9
gay travelers 133-4, *see also* Play *subindex*
Glitter Gulch 9
Golden Gate 55
Golden Nugget 56
Goodman, Oscar 153
government 153-4
Grand Canyon 145

H
Hard Rock 56-7
health 166
history 151-3
holidays 127, 166
Hooters 57
Hoover Dam 144
hotels 26, 164
Hughes, Howard 152

I
Imperial Palace 57
internet access 166-7
internet resources 166-7
 accommodation 163, 165
itineraries 27-31

J
jewelry 82-3, see also Shop
 subindex

K
karaoke 139

L
Lake Mead National
 Recreation Area 144
legal matters 156
lesbian travelers 133-4, see
 also Play subindex
live music 125-8, see also Play
 subindex
 festivals 127
Lost City Museum 144
Luxor 47

M
magazines 167-8
magic shows 139-41, see
 also Play subindex
malls 80-2, see also Shop
 subindex

000 map pages

Mandalay Bay 48
marriage, see weddings
McGhie's Bike Outpost 146
MGM Grand 40-1
Mirage 42
mobile phones 168
money 165-6, 167, see
 also costs
monorail travel 162, **192**
Monte Carlo 57
motorcycle travel 161, 162
museums 66-8, see also See
 subindex
music 125-8, 158, see
 also Shop & Play subindexes

N
Naked City 9, **186-7**
neighborhoods 9
Nevada Test Site 152, 154
New York-New York 49
newspapers 167-8
Newton, Wayne 16
nightclubs 21, 130-3, see
 also Play subindex
nightlife 119-42, see also Play
 subindex

O
organized tours 148, 168
Orleans 57-8

P
Palms 58
Paris-Las Vegas 50
parking 162
passports 161
photography 168
Planet Hollywood 58
planning 30, 165-6
Plaza 58-9
poker 35
 festivals 127
 rooms 36

police 166
politics 153-4
pollution 154-5
pools 15
population 155
production shows 136-9, see
 also Play subindex
prostitution 155, 156
Puck, Wolfgang 91, 94,
 99, 106

R
Rainbow Vista 144
Rat Pack 152, 157, 158
Red Rock 59
Red Rock Canyon 146-7
restaurants 91-117, see
 also Eat subindex
Richard Meltzer 157
rides 68-70, see also See
 subindex
Rio 60
roulette 36

S
Sahara 51
Sam's Town 60
shopping 79-89, See
 also Shop subindex
shows 136-9, see also Play
 subindex
Siegel, Benjamin 'Bugsy' 152
sights 65-77
 free 30-1
Silica Dome 144
Silvertown 60
slot machines 37
smoking 156
souvenirs 18
spas 20, 123-5, see also Play
 subindex
sports 142, 156
 books 37

Spring Mountain Ranch State
   Park 146
Star Trek 88, 122, 123
steakhouses 97, *see also* Eat
   subindex
Stratosphere 52
Stratosphere Tower 22-3
Strip, the 9, 12, **180**, **182**
strip clubs 134-6, *see also* Play
   subindex
swimming pools 15

T

taxis 163
telephone services 168-9
Thompson, Hunter S 157
TI (Treasure Island) 53
tickets 119, 142
tipping 169
Tom Wolfe 157
tourist information 169
tours 168
   outfitters 148
tram travel 162
transportation 160-3
trolley travel 163
Tropicana 60
TV 158-9

U

ultra lounges 128-30, *see
   also* Play *subindex*
University of Nevada 9, **190-1**

V

vacations 166
Valley of Fire 144
Vegas Club 61
Venetian 43
venues 141
video 168
video poker 37
visas 161

W

weddings 24-5, 76-7, *see also*
   See *subindex*
   chapels 24, 76-7
Westside 9, **188-9**
White Domes 144
wildlife 72-5, *see also* See
   subindex
Willow Springs 146
Wynn, Steve 153, 157
Wynn 44

Y

Yucca Mountain 154

CASINOS

Bally's 54
Bellagio 38
Binion's 45
Caesars Palace 39
California 54
Circus Circus 54
El Cortez 54-5
Ellis Island 139
Excalibur 55
Flamingo 46
Golden Gate 55
Golden Nugget 56
Hard Rock 56-7
Hooters 57
Imperial Palace 57
Luxor 47
Mandalay Bay 48
MGM Grand 40-1
Mirage 42
Monte Carlo 57
New York-New York 49
Orleans 57-8
Palms 58
Paris-Las Vegas 50
Planet Hollywood 58
Plaza 58-9
Red Rock 59

Rio 60
Sahara 51
Sam's Town 60
Silvertown 60
Stratosphere 52
TI (Treasure Island) 53
Tropicana 60
Vegas Club 61
Venetian 43
Wynn 44

SEE

Gardens & Wildlife
Bellagio Conservatory &
   Botanical Gardens 72
Flamingo Wildlife Habitat 72
Lion Habitat at MGM Grand 72
Mirage Casino Hotel 72-3
Shark Reef 73
Siegfried & Roy's Secret
   Garden & Dolphin Habitat
   73-4

Museums & Art Galleries
Arts Factory 66
Atomic Testing Museum 66
Bellagio Gallery of Fine Art 67
Commerce Street Studios 67
Guggenheim Hermitage
   Museum 67
Hard Rock 67
King Tut Museum 67
Las Vegas Art Museum 68
Main Street Station 68
Wynn Collection 68

Quirky Las Vegas
Imperial Palace
   Dealertainers 75
Liberace Museum 75
Madame Tussauds Las
   Vegas 75

Museum of the American
  Cocktail 75
Neon Museum 76
Pinball Hall of Fame 76
Slots-A-Fun 76
Star Trek: The Experience 76

Spectacles
Circus Circus Midway 70
Fountains of Bellagio 71
Freemont Street
  Experience 71
Mirage Casino Hotel 72-3
Mirage Volcano 71-2
Siegfried & Roy's Secret
  Garden & Dolphin
  Habitat 73-4
Sirens of TI 72

Thrill Rides &
Amusements
Adventuredome 68
Eiffel Tower Experience 68-9
ESPN Zone Sports Arena 69
Gameworks 69
Las Vegas Cyber Speedway &
  Speed 69
Manhattan Express 69-70
Richard Petty Driving
  Experience 70
Stratosphere Tower 70
Venetian Gondolas 70

Wedding Chapels
A Special Memory Wedding
  Chapel 77
Graceland Wedding Chapel 77
Little Church of the West 77
Maverick Helicopters 77
Viva Las Vegas Weddings 77
Wee Kirk O' The Heather 77

000 map pages

LAS VEGAS >174

SHOP
Clothing & Jewelry
Attic 82
Buffalo Exchange 82
D'Loe House of Style 82
Fred Leighton 83
Valentino's Zootsuit
  Connection 83
Williams Costume Company 83

Music & Books
Alternate Reality Comics 83-4
Gambler's Book Shop 84
Reading Room 84
Zia Records 84-5

Adult Stores
Adult Superstore 87
Bad Attitude Boutique 87
Bare Essentials/Fantasy
  Fashion 87
Paradise Electro
  Stimulations 87
Red Shoes 87
Slightly Sinful 87
Strings of Las Vegas 87-8

Shopping Malls & Arcades
Fashion Outlet Mall 81
Fashion Show 80
Forum Shops 80
Grand Canal Shoppes 80
Hard Rock 80-1
Las Vegas Premium Outlets 81
Mandalay Place 81
Miracle Mile Shops 81
Via Bellagio 81-2
Wynn Esplanade 82

Specialist Stores
55° Wine + Design 85-6
Antiques District 85
Auto Collections 85
Casa Fuente 85
Exotic Cars 85

Funk House 85
Gypsy Caravan 85
Houdini's Magic Shop 86
Metropolitan Museum of Art
  Store 86
Niketown 86
Red Rooster Antique Mall 86-7

Weird & Wonderful
Bonanza Gifts 88
Deep Space Nine
  Promenade 88
Gamblers General Store 88
Gun Store 88
Rainbow Feather Co 88-9
Serge's Showgirl Wigs 89
Showcase Slots 89

EAT

Bakeries
Il Fornaio Paneterriaa 101

Barbecue
Salt Lick BBQ 115

Buffets
Buffet 92
Carnival World & Village
  Seafood Buffets 114
Sterling Brunch 92

Cajun
Commander's Palace 102-3
Emeril's 98
Rosemary's 115

Cal-Italian
Postrio 106
Wolfgang Puck Bar & Grill
  99-100

Chinese
Fin 100
Lillie's Noodle House 108
Ping Pang Pong 115

Chinese Fusion
Chinois 94

Comfort Food
Burger Bar 96
Hash House A Go Go 114
Roxy's Diner 103

Continental
Alizé 113
Top of the World 103

Creole
Commander's Palace 102-3
Emeril's 98

Cuban
Florida Café 108

Delis
'Witchcraft 99
Canter's Deli 103-4
Paymon's Mediterranean Cafe 112-13

Eclectic
Simon Kitchen & Bar 113

Fast Food
Cypress Street Marketplace 94-5
In-N-Out Burger 114-15
Luv-It Frozen Custard 108-9
Mahalo Express 109
Mermaids 109
Village Eateries 101

French
Alex 106-7
Alizé 113
Bouchon 105
Daniel Boulud Brasserie 107
Eiffel Tower Restaurant 102
Fleur de Lys 97
Joël Robuchon 98-9
Le Cirque 93
Le Village Buffet 102

Lutèce 105-6
Mon Ami Gabi 102
Picasso 93
Restaurant Guy Savoy 95

French-Californian
Pinot Brasserie 106

Fusion
Firefly 111
Sensi 94

Hawaiian
Mahalo Express 109

Indian
Origin India 112

Italian
Bartolotta Ristorante di Mare 107
Canaletto 105
Circo 92
Il Fornaio 101
Sazio 117
Zeffirino 106

Japanese
Japonais 100-1

Japanese Fusion
Nobu 112
Okada 107
Shibuya 99
Social House 104-5

Mediterranean
Alex 106-7
Olives 93
Paymon's Mediterranean Cafe 112-13
Picasso 93

Mexican
Garduño's 114
Isla Mexican Kitchen & Tequila Bar 104
Pink Taco 113

New American
Aureole 96
Bradley Ogden 94
Fix 92
Rosemary's 115
Table 34 117
Tableau 108

Pan-Asian
Lillie's Noodle House 108
Red & Asian Bistro 107
Social House 104-5
Todai 103

Pizza
Metro Pizza 111-12

Pub Grub
Monte Carlo Pub & Brewery 101

Russian
Red Square 97

Seafood
Bartolotta Ristorante di Mare 107
Bouchon 105
Carnival World & Village Seafood Buffets 114
Craftsteak 98
Emeril's 98
Le Village Buffet 102
Mon Ami Gabi 102
Prime Steakhouse 94
RM 98
San Francisco Shrimp Bar & Deli 109-10
Seablue 99
Second Street Grill 110
Todai 103
Triple George Grill 110

Southwestern
Isla Mexican Kitchen & Tequila Bar 104

Mesa Grill 95

Steakhouses
Binion's Ranch Steakhouse 108
Capital Grille 96
Charlie Palmer Steak 96-7
Craftsteak 98
Delmonico Steakhouse 105
Envy 110-11
Golden Steer 114
N9NE 115
Prime Steakhouse 94
Pullman Bar & Grille 109
Redwood Bar & Grille 109
Second Street Grill 110
SW Steakhouse 107-8
Triple George Grill 110

Tapas
Firefly 111

Thai
Cafe Ba-Ba-Reeba 96
Lotus of Siam 111

Vietnamese
Pho at the Coffee Shop 104

PLAY
Bars
Art Bar 120
Beauty Bar 120
Carnaval Court 120
ESPN Zone 120
Fireside Lounge 120-1
Hofbräuhaus 121
Hookah Lounge 121
Napoleon's 121
Quark's Bar 123
Triple 7 123

Cinemas

Brenden Palms Casino 141
Las Vegas Drive-In 141
Luxor Imax Theatre 141-2
Regal Village Square 142

Comedy & Magic
Comedy Stop 139
Improv 139
Lance Burton: Master
  Magician 139
Penn & Teller 140
Second City 140
World's Greatest Magic show
  140-1

Gay & Lesbian Venues
Buffalo 133
Charlie's 133
Free Zone 133
Gipsy 133
Goodtimes 133-4
Kräve 134
La Cage 134
Piranha 134
Suede 134
Toucan's Bar & Grille 134

Live Music
Brendan's Irish Pub 125
Bunkhouse Saloon 125
Double Down Saloon 126
House of Blues 126
Joint 126
Las Vegas Hilton 125
Matteo's Underground
  Lounge 128
Sand Dollar Blues Lounge 128

Nightclubs
Body English 130-1
Empire Ballroom 131
Foundation Room 131
Ice 131
Jet 131
Lights 131-2

OPM 132
Pure 132
Rain 132
Tao 132-3

Production Shows
Beacher's Madhouse 136
Fashionistas 136
Folies Bergère 137
Jubilee! 137
Kà 137
La Femme 137
Legends in Concert 137
Love 138
Mystère 138
O 138-9

Spas
Bathhouse 123
Canyon Ranch Spaclub 124
Oasis Spa 124
Palms Spa & Amp Salon 124
Red Rock Spa 124
Spa by Mandara 125

Strip Clubs
Chippendales Theater 135
Club Paradise 135
Girls of Glitter Gulch 135
Olympic Gardens 135
Sapphire 135-6
Seamless 136
Thunder Down Under 135

**Ultra Lounges &
After-Hours Venues**
Drai's 128
Forty Deuce 128
Ghostbar 128
Mix 129
Pussycat Dolls Lounge 129
Romance at Top of the
  World 129
Tabú 129
Tangerine 130
V Bar 130

000 map pages

A B C D

599

Kirkland Ave

Loch Lomond Ave

Highland Ave

Western St

Chicago Ave

Fairfield Ave

S Main St

604

599

St Louis Ave

11 🏛

🏛 **21**

See Naked Ca
Map pp186–

Boston Ave

🏛 **12**

Baltimore Ave

Industrial Rd

Tam Dr

Cleveland Ave

Paradise Rd

589

See Westside Map (pp188–9)

W Sahara Ave

Cincinnati Ave

🏛 **18**

See UNIV & Eastside Map (pp190–

16 🏛

589

E Sahara Ave

Teddy Dr

Kings Way

15

🏛 **8**

Sahara
Monorail
Station

🏛 **3**

605

Karen Ave

Highland Dr

Industrial Rd

Westwood Dr

Circus Circus Dr

🏛 **1**

S Las Vegas Blvd (The Strip)

🏛 **2**

10 🏛

Riviera Blvd

Riviera

Las Vegas
Hilton Monorail
Station

• Post Office

⭐ **22**

Kishner Dr

⭐ **19**

Stardust

Convention Center Dr

Mel Ave

Las Vegas
Convention
Center
Monorail
Station

Stardust Rd

• Greek
Isles

Desert Inn Super Arterial

Western Ave

Fashion Show Dr

17 🏛

🏛 **15**

Sierra Vista L

• American Express

Wynn Golf
Course &
Country Club

Edison

Spring Mountain Rd

S Las Vegas Blvd (The Strip)

Vegas Plaza Dr

🏛 **13**

Burbank Ave

Sands Ave

Elm Dr

Country Club La

Twain Av

Manhattan St

Paradise Rd

Cassella La

Pershing Rd

🏛 **14**

605

🏛 **6**

🏛 **7**

⭐ **20**

Millenium
• Foto

🏛 **4**

Harrah's/Imperial
Palace Monorail
Station

Koval La

Westchester Dr

See The Strip - South Map (p182)

🏛 **9**

604

🏛 **5**

**THE
STRIP**

Ida Ave

Winnick Ave

Flamingo Wash

Chicago Ave

A

B

C

1

2

3

4

5

6

0   500 m
0   0.3 miles

⊙ SEE

Adventuredome......**1** B3
Circus Circus **2** C3
GM–The Drive **3** D2
Guggenheim
Hermitage Museum (see 14)
Harrah's **4** B6
Imperial Palace **5** B6
Las Vegas Cyber
Speedway............... (see 8)
Madame Tussauds
Las Vegas................ (see 14)
Midway................... (see 2)
Mirage **6** A6
Mirage Volcano **7** B6
Sahara **8** D2
Siegfried & Roy's
Secret Garden &
Dolphin Habitat **9** A6
Sirens of TI,.... .... (see 13)
Slots-A-Fun ,...........**10** C3
Stratosphere **11** D1
Stratosphere Tower.**12** D1
TI (Treasure Island) .**13** B5
Venetian..................**14** B6
Venetian Gondolas.. (see 14)
Wynn **15** C5

▢ SHOP

Auto Collection .... (see 5)
Bonanza Gifts..........**16** D2

▥ EAT

Alex .... (see 15)
Bartoletto
Ristorante di Mare. (see 15)
Bouchon .... (see 14)
Café Ba-Ra-Recba!.. (see 17)
Canaletto................. (see 14)
Canter's Deli .... (see 13)
Capital Grille .... (see 17)
Daniel Boulud
Brasserie.. .... (see 15)
Delmonico
Steakhouse............... (see 14)
Fin........................... (see 6)
Golden Steer,..... . **18** C2
Isla Mexican
Kitchen & Tequila
Bar........................... (see 13)
Japonais .... (see 6)
Lutèce..................... (see 14)
Okada .... (see 15)
Pho at the Coffee
Shop .... (see 13)
Pinot Brasserie........ (see 14)
Postrio..................... (see 14)
Red 8 Asian Bistro ... (see 15)
Roxy's Diner .... (see 11)
SW Steakhouse .... (see 15)
Social House............ (see 13)
Tableau.................... (see 15)
Top of the World...... (see 11)
Zefferino .... (see 14)

★ PLAY

Canyon Ranch SpaClub
(see 14)
Carnaval Court .... (see 4)
Fireside Lounge.......**19** C3
The Improv **20** B6
Jet........................... (see 6)
Legends in Concert . (see 5)
Love........................ (see 6)
Mystère .... (see 13)
Piano Bar.... ...... (see 4)
Romance at Top of
the World................**21** D1
Tangerine .... (see 13)
Tao.......................... (see 14)
Tix 4 Tonight........... (see 17)
Tix 4 Tonight...........**22** C3
V Bar....................... (see 14)

THE STRIP - SOUTH

🔵 SEE

Bally's 1   C2
Bellagio 2   B2
Bellagio Gallery of
Fine Art .... (see 2)
Caesars Palace 3   B1
ESPN Zone .... (see 15)
Eiffel Tower
Experience 4   B2
Excalibur 5   B4
Flamingo 6   B1
Flamingo Wildlife
Habitat .... (see 6)
Fountains of
Bellagio 7   B2
GameWorks 8   B3
Hooters 9   C4
King Tut Museum .... (see 11)
Lion Habitat .... (see 13)
Little Church of
the West 10   B6
Luxor 11   B5
Mandalay Bay 12   B5
Manhattan Express .. (see 15)
MGM Grand 13   B4
Monte Carlo 14   B3
Museum of the
American Cocktail .. (see 21)
New York-New York 15   B4
Paris-Las Vegas 16   C2
Planet Hollywood ... 17   C2
Shark Reef .... (see 12)
THEhotel at
Mandalay Bay .... (see 12)
Tropicana 18   C4

🛍 SHOP

55° Wine + Design .. (see 20)
Casa Fuente .... (see 3)
Exotic Cars .... (see 19)
Forum Shops ... 19   B1
Fred Leighton .... (see 2)
Houdini's Magic
Shop .... (see 19)
Mandalay Place 20   B5
Metropolitan Museum
of Art Store .... (see 21)

Miracle Mile Shops .. 21   C2
Niketown .... (see 19)
Reading Room .... (see 20)
Via Bellagio .... (see 2)

🍴 EAT

Aureole .... (see 12)
Bertolini's .... (see 3)
Bradley Ogden .... (see 3)
Buffet at Bellagio .... (see 2)
Burger Bar .... (see 20)
Charlie Palmer
Steak .... (see 12)
Chinois .... (see 3)
Circo .... (see 2)
Commander's
Palace .... (see 21)
Craftsteak .... (see 13)
Cypress Street
Marketplace .... (see 3)
Eiffel Tower
Restaurant .... (see 16)
Emeril's .... (see 15)
Fix .... (see 2)
Fleur de Lys .... (see 12)
Il Fornaio . ... (see 15)
Joël Robuchon .... (see 13)
Le Cirque .... (see 2)
Le Village Buffet ..... (see 16)
Mesa Grill .... (see 3)
Mon Ami Gabi .... (see 16)
Monte Carlo Pub &
Brewery .... (see 14)
Olives .... (see 2)
Picasso .. .. (see 2)
Prime Steakhouse .... (see 2)
RM .... (see 12)
Red Square .... (see 12)
Restaurant Guy
Savoy .... (see 3)
SeaBlue .... (see 13)
Sensi .... (see 2)
Shibuya .... (see 13)
Sterling Brunch .... (see 1)
Todai .... (see 21)
Village Eateries .... (see 15)
'Wichcraft .... (see 13)

Wolfgang Puck
Bar & Grill .... (see 13)

⭐ PLAY

Bathhouse .... (see 12)
Coca-Cola Tickets
2Nite 22   B3
Comedy Stop .... (see 18)
Drai's 23   B1
Empire Ballroom 24   B3
Fix .... (see 2)
Folies Bergère .... (see 18)
Fontana Bar .... (see 2)
Forty Deuce .... (see 20)
Foundation Room ... (see 12)
House of Blues .... (see 12)
Ice 25   D3
Jubilee! .... (see 1)
Krave .... (see 21)
Kà .... (see 13)
La Femme .... (see 13)
Lance Burton:
Master Magician .... (see 14)
Light .... (see 2)
Luxor IMAX Theatre (see 11)
MGM Grand Garden
Arena .... (see 13)
Mandalay Bay
Events Center .... (see 12)
Mix .... (see 12)
Monte Carlo Pub &
Brewery .... (see 14)
Napoleon's .... (see 16)
O .... (see 2)
OPM .... (see 19)
Oasis Spa .... (see 11)
Pure .... (see 3)
Pussycat Dolls Lounge
(see 3)
Red Square .... (see 12)
Second City .... (see 6)
Spa by Mandarin ...... (see 16)
Tabú .... (see 13)
rumjungle ... . (see 12)
Thunder Down
Under 26   B4
Tix 4 Tonight 27   B3

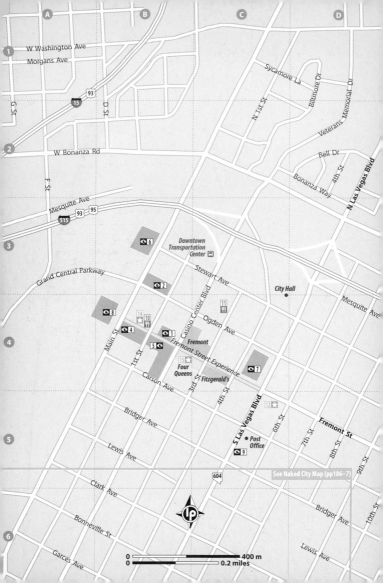

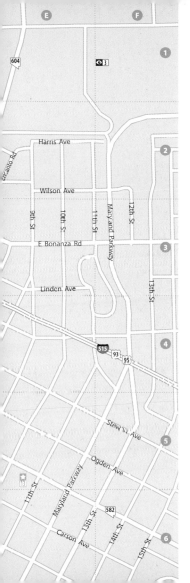

DOWNTOWN

👁 SEE

Binion's	1	B4
California	2	B3
Cashman Field	3	F1
Golden Gate	4	B4
Golden Nugget	5	B4
Main Street Station	6	B3
Neon Museum	(see 7)	
Neonopolis	7	C4
Plaza	8	B4
Wee Kirk O' the Heather	9	C5

🍴 EAT

Binion's Ranch Steakhouse	(see 1)	
Lillie's Noodle House	(see 5)	
Mermaids	10	B4
Pullman Bar & Grille	(see 6)	
Redwood Bar & Grille	(see 2)	
San Francisco Shrimp Bar & Deli	(see 4)	
Triple George Grill	11	C4

⭐ PLAY

Beauty Bar	12	C5
Bunkhouse Saloon	13	E5
Girls of Glitter Gulch	14	B4
Sidebar	(see 11)	
Tix 4 Tonight	15	B4
Triple 7	(see 6)	

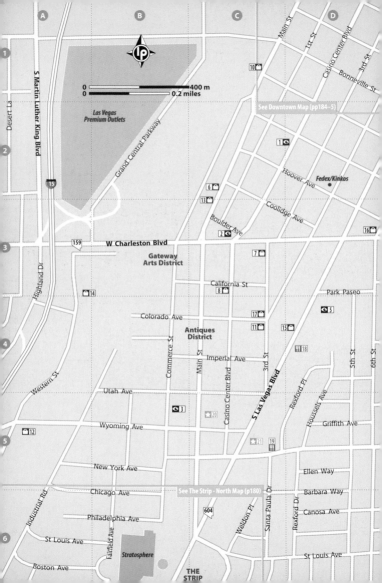

A B C D

1

2

3

4

5

6

S Martin Luther King Blvd

Desert La

I-15

Las Vegas Premium Outlets

Grand Central Parkway

Main St

1st St

Casino Center Blvd

3rd St

10

Bonneville St

See Downtown Map (pp184–5)

1

Hoover Ave

Fedex/Kinkos

6

13

Coolidge Ave

Boulder Ave

2

16

159

W Charleston Blvd

7

Gateway Arts District

Highland Dr

14

California St

8

Park Paseo

17

5

Colorado Ave

11

15

Antiques District

18

Western St

Commerce St

Main St

Imperial Ave

Casino Center Blvd

3rd St

S Las Vegas Blvd

Rexford Pl

Houssels Ave

5th St

6th St

Griffith Ave

Utah Ave

3

20

12

Wyoming Ave

21

19

Ellen Way

New York Ave

Barbara Way

Industrial Rd

Chicago Ave

See The Strip - North Map (p180)

Rexford Dr

Santa Paula Dr

Weldon Dr

Canosa Ave

604

Fairfield Ave

Philadelphia Ave

St Louis Ave

St Louis Ave

Boston Ave

Stratosphere

THE STRIP

0 ———————— 400 m
0 ———————— 0.2 miles

NAKED CITY

⊙ SEE

A Special Memory Wedding Chapel	1	D2
Arts Factory	2	C3
Commerce Street Studios	3	B5
Graceland Wedding Chapel	4	E2
Viva Las Vegas Weddings	5	D4

🛍 SHOP

Attic	6	C2
D'Loe House of Style	7	C3
Funk House	8	C3
Gambler's Book Shop	9	F3
Gamblers General Store	10	C1
Gypsy Caravan	11	C4
Paradise Electro Stimulations	12	A5
Rainbow Feather Co	13	C3
Red Rooster Antique Mall	14	A3
Slightly Sinful	15	D4
Valentino's Zootsuit Connection	16	D3
Williams Costume Company	17	C4

🍴 EAT

Florida Café	18	D4
Luv-It Frozen Custard	19	C5

⭐ PLAY

Art Bar	20	C5
Olympic Garden	21	C5

WESTSIDE

🌀 SEE

Orleans	1	C6
Palms	2	D4
Rio	3	E4

🏠 SHOP

Adult Superstore	4	D6
Bare Essentials	5	D1
Fantasy Fashions	(see 5)	
Interstate Records	6	C5
Showcase Slots	7	F1
Strings of Las Vegas	8	D6

🍴 EAT

Carnival World Buffet	(see 3)	
Garduños	(see 2)	
In N Out Burger	9	E6
N9NE Steakhouse	(see 2)	
Ping Pang Pong	10	D4
Sazio	(see 1)	
Village Seafood Buffet	(see 3)	

⭐ PLAY

Brendan's Irish Pub	(see 1)	
Brenden Palms Casino	(see 2)	
Charlie's	11	D6
Chippendales Theater	(see 3)	
ghostbar	(see 2)	
Orleans Arena	(see 1)	
Palms Spa & Amp Salon	(see 2)	
Penn & Teller	(see 3)	
Rain	(see 2)	
Sand Dollar Blues Lounge	12	E3
Seamless	13	D6

UNLV & EASTSIDE

SEE

Atomic Testing Museum	1	C4
Commercial Center	2	C1
Deep Space Nine Promenade	(see 25)	
Hard Rock	3	B5
Liberace Museum	4	D6
Star Trek: The Experience	(see 25)	

SHOP

Alternate Reality Comics	5	D5
Buffalo Exchange	6	D4
Deep Space Nine Promenade	(see 25)	
Get Booked	7	B5
Gun Store	8	F6
Hard Rock	(see 3)	
Serge's Showgirl Wigs	(see 12)	
Zia Records	9	E4

EAT

Envy	10	B3
Firefly	11	B4
Lotus of Siam	12	C1
Metro Pizza	13	D6
Nobu	(see 3)	
Origin India	14	B5
Paymon's Mediterranean Café	15	C4
Pink Taco	(see 3)	
Simon Kitchen & Bar	(see 3)	

PLAY

Beacher's Madhouse	(see 3)	
Body English	(see 3)	
Buffalo	16	B5
Club Paradise	17	B5
Double Down Saloon	18	B5
Ellis Island Casino	19	B4
FreeZone	20	B5
Gipsy	21	B5
Goodtimes	22	D6
Hofbräuhaus	23	B5
Hookah Lounge	24	C4
The Joint	(see 3)	
Las Vegas Hilton	25	B2
Piranha	26	B5
Quark's Bar	(see 25)	
Rock Spa	(see 3)	
Suede	27	B5
Toucan's Bar & Grille	28	B5

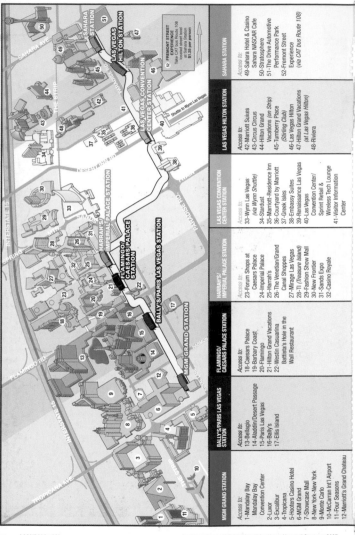

MGM GRAND STATION

Access to:
1–Mandalay Bay
Mandalay Bay
Convention Center
2–Luxor
3–Excalibur
4–Tropicana
5–Hooters Casino Hotel
6–MGM Grand
7–Showcase Mall
8–New York-New York
9–Monte Carlo
10–McCarran Int'l Airport
11–Four Seasons
12–Marriott's Grand Chateau

BALLY'S/PARIS LAS VEGAS STATION

Access to:
13–Bellagio
14–Aladdin/Desert Passage
15–Paris Las Vegas
16–Bally's
17–Ellis Island

FLAMINGO/CAESARS PALACE STATION

Access to:
18–Caesars Palace
19–Barbary Coast
20–Flamingo
21–Hilton Grand Vacations
22–Westin Casuarina
Battista's Hole in the
Wall Restaurant

HARRAH'S/IMPERIAL PALACE STATION

Access to:
23–Forum Shops at
Caesars Palace
24–Imperial Palace
25–Harrah's
26–The Venetian/Grand
Canal Shoppes
27–Mirage Las Vegas
28–TI (Treasure Island)
29–Fashion Show Mall
30–New Frontier
31–Sands Expo
32–Casino Royale

LAS VEGAS CONVENTION CENTER STATION

Access to:
33–Wynn Las Vegas
(via Wynn Shuttle)
34–Stardust
35–Marriott-Residence Inn
36–Courtyard by Marriott
37–Greek Isles
38–Embassy Suites
39–Renaissance Las Vegas
40–Las Vegas
Convention Center/
Sprint Retail &
Wireless Tech Lounge
41–Visitor Information
Center

LAS VEGAS HILTON STATION

Access to:
42–Marriott Suites
43–Circus Circus
44–Hilton Grand
45–Turnberry Place
(String Club)
46–Las Vegas Hilton
47–Hilton Grand Vacations
(at Las Vegas Hilton)
48–Riviera

SAHARA STATION

Access to:
49–Sahara Hotel & Casino
Sahara NASCAR Cafe
50–Stratosphere
51–The Drive Automotive
Performance Park
52–Fremont Street
Experience
(via CAT bus Route 108)

52 FREMONT STREET
EXPERIENCE
Take CAT bus Route 108
located street level
at Sahara Station
$1.25 per person

Las Vegas Monorail Route Map © Las Vegas Monorail Company 2007